Critical Guides to French Texts

Critical Guides to French Texts

EDITED BY ROGER LITTLE, WOLFGANG VAN EMDEN, DAVID WILLIAMS

La Chanson de Roland

Wolfgang van Emden

Professor of French,
University of Reading

Grant & Cutler Ltd
1995

© Grant & Cutler Ltd 1995

ISBN 0 7293 0386 1

Printed in Spain by
Artes Gráficas Soler, S.A., Valencia
for
GRANT & CUTLER LTD
55-57 GREAT MARLBOROUGH STREET, LONDON WIV 2AY

Contents

Foreword

La Chanson de Roland has long been, and remains, one of the most controversial, as well as one of the greatest, works of French literature. Controversy rages, for example, about its very nature: how did the destruction of Charlemagne's baggage-train, with the probable death, among others, of one Roland, Lord of the Breton Marches, at the hands of Christian Basques on 15 August 778 (see *1*,[*] pp.xii-xiii) become the epic confrontation of Christianity and Islam of our poem, more than three centuries later? Does the extant *Chanson de Roland* belong to what is known, in something of an oxymoron, as 'oral literature', or was it written down in the same way as the *Aeneid* or *Paradise Lost*, or indeed mediaeval romances like those of Chrétien de Troyes?

What, to raise a second area of debate, are we to make of its hero, Roland? Do we see him as an exemplary figure, a saint who sacrifices himself to ensure the proper completion of the holy war which his uncle, Charlemagne, has been fighting in Spain? Do we see him as an exemplary hero in an opposite sense: the perfect feudal vassal in a poem whose ethos is basically pagan (this is often linked with the Germanic prehistory of the Franks), one who carries out his duty perfectly and, like the saint, has no reason to regret any of his decisions or actions? Or do we see him as a tragic hero, magnificent but flawed in an almost Aristotelian sense, who brings about the disaster of Roncevaux by his own fault, and achieves sainthood only by reversing his earlier decisions when he realises what their effect has been, and repents?

These are the two main areas of controversy on which I had originally planned to concentrate in this volume. Given problems of

---

[*] Italicised numerals, followed, where appropriate, by a page number, refer to the items in the Bibliography at the end of this volume.

space, I must in the event do no more than state my own
conclusions on the mode of composition, referring briefly to the
issues involved and the scholars to be consulted, in the Introduction,
and concentrate on the question of interpretation in the close
reading which will form the bulk of this monograph.

Even on this latter aspect, I would not wish controversy to be
the main theme of the book, and I shall therefore refer the reader to
representative proponents of other exegeses without spending
inordinate time in attempting to 'refute' their arguments here. (I
shall also comment on other matters of interest as they present
themselves.) On my main theme, the presentation of the text will
offer a personal but, I hope, a coherent exegesis, which should be
seen as one of several possible approaches. It is characteristic of
great literature that it often provokes conflicting interpretations.

In preparing this volume I have used the recent re-issue by
T.D. Hemming (Bibliography, *1*) of Frederick Whitehead's classic
edition of *La Chanson de Roland* (*2*). The latter has been used by
generations of British students, and gives a conservative and
soundly edited version of the poem; Hemming has justifiably made
minor textual emendations and provided a new introduction and
helpful notes, especially designed for students. There are many
other editions, with and without translations into modern French or
English, some of which are listed in the Bibliography.

I shall assume the reader to have the Hemming/Whitehead or
the Whitehead edition (or another with the same line-numbering)
open next to this monograph: given limited space, there will be few
quotations but many references. Hemming admirably sets the poem
in its historical and literary context, and I have as far as possible
avoided going over these aspects again. Finally, it should always be
remembered that we have a single surviving manuscript out of an
unknown number of copies; there is no way of returning to the
autograph of the author, if (as I believe) such a thing existed, and
our copy is certainly flawed in places. Caution is therefore necessary
in founding arguments on small details of the text, particularly
where formulaic expressions or words appearing at the end of the

line, providing the required assonance, are concerned. I have sought to exercise that caution, and hope readers will do so too.

My thanks are due to Mr Raymond Howard of Grant and Cutler Limited, for encouraging me both to begin and to complete this project, and for allowing me exceptionally to exceed the normal word-limit used for this series; also and especially to my friend and colleague Dr Karen Pratt, of King's College, London, who kindly read a late draft of this monograph, made many valuable observations and played devil's advocate on a number of my arguments; to my wife Joan, for reading the same draft from a less specialised point of view, and with a stylist's eye; finally to my fellow Editor in this series, Professor Roger Little, who read and commented on the last draft with his customary thoroughness and erudition. Since I have used some, but not all, of my colleagues' suggestions, I remain very much responsible for what follows, and particularly for anything that may be controversial.

1. Introduction: what kind of epic?

The one surviving copy of *La Chanson de Roland*, in the form which concerns us, is Manuscript Digby 23 of the Bodleian Library in Oxford, dating from the second quarter of the twelfth century according to most current opinion: Hemming, *1*, p.xxix, following Samaran, *141*, pp.523-27, as do e.g. Le Gentil, *101*, p.8, Moignet, *8*, p.10, Segre, *6*, Vol. I, p.47; Short, *9*, p.10, *143* (referring to Bédier and others) and Burgess, *12*, p.7, both consider it may be as late as 1170. It was copied by an Anglo-Norman scribe, though the poet was a continental Western French speaker. For the later versions, in French – especially the late twelfth-century *Rhymed Roland* – and other languages, see Bédier (*32*, pp.65-240), Segre (*6*, vol.I, pp.15-22), Hemming (*1*, pp.xxx-xxxi). All the non-Oxford witnesses are descended from one lost version, while the Digby manuscript, *O*, stands in a different, and generally less corrupt (*6*, vol. I, p.15), line of descent from the original.

The poem itself, in the Digby version, is dated by most scholars to the very end of the eleventh or the beginning of the twelfth century (Le Gentil, *101*, pp.22-31 for opinions up to 1968; Bender, *33*, pp.26-27; Vance, *152*, pp.9, 95; Duggan, *55*, p.1; Cook, *50*, p.xvii; Hemming, *1*, xvi-xvii for recent opinions; Zink, *172*, p.87). The main arguments are based on the influence of certain aspects of the First Crusade and of other battles against the Saracens around the end of the eleventh century, archaic aspects of the language, and the date generally assigned to the manuscript. This last would tend automatically to rule out the recent efforts of H.-E. Keller (*92*, echoing, for contrasting reasons, Mireaux, *111*) to date most of contents of the poem to the middle of the twelfth century, and the Oxford version itself to 1170; the arguments are based on Capetian political involvement with Saint Denis and its abbot Suger, and I have expressed my reservations on their strength in my review of *Autour de Roland* (*163*; cf. Hemming, *81*; recently however Mickel, *110*, pp.4ff. and n.9; this book's conclusions are open to the same objection, and others).

In any case, everyone is agreed that there were earlier versions of the subject, oral or written, so that much, if not all, of the poet's narrative material was available to him in his source(s). We cannot measure what he brought to the contents of the story, but we can hope to judge what he has made of it in literary terms, and the qualities of this particular version, provided we see it *being* a particular version, as the work of an individual author.

This is the subject of controversy. The *Chanson de Roland*, intended, like all *chansons de geste*, for singing (see Hemming, *1*, x-xi, Suard, *148*, pp.12-13), is composed in very flexible units. Largely end-stopped ('paratactic') lines, each composed of two hemistichs (of four and six syllables, respectively before and after a pause or 'caesura'), are grouped in irregular stanzas, '*laisses*' (this word will not be italicised elsewhere). Each *Roland* laisse is on one assonance (as distinct from the rhyme of many later epics, which is more difficult to find) and the poet continues on that assonance until he wishes to start a new laisse. Hemistichs, being largely self-contained, can in principle easily become interchangeable formulae, allowing the creation of lines with great economy of effort, and the whole system would certainly appear to lend itself readily to improvisation.

Many scholars argue, mainly from its formulaic style, that Old French epic does belong to the field of 'oral literature'. In orally composed epic, such as the well-researched Serbo-Croatian tradition, there is no fixed text of any subject; poets learn in their training to reproduce the story line by using a traditional system of formulae, each of which may be defined as 'a group of words which is regularly employed under the same metrical conditions to express a given essential idea' (Lord, *104*, p.4). In practice, this usually means a hemistich which is repeated at least once within a given poem (Duggan, *55*, p.10), though this simplification of the Lord definition cuts out certain groups of words which do not fill a hemistich. Even by this second criterion, Duggan shows the *Roland*

to be 35.2% formulaic (*55*, p.34), well above the 20% limit which
he assigns, on the basis of comparisons between various types of
poem, to written literature. A more syntactic model of the formula
(see Heinemann, *79*, cf. Kay, *91*; Raymond Eichmann, *62*, pp.97-109,
esp. p.100) would certainly increase the percentage considerably.

   On the demonstrable basis that genuine oral epic, such as the
Serbo-Croatian corpus recorded and analysed by Parry and Lord
(*124*), is necessarily highly formulaic, 'traditionalists' of this school
of thought conclude that the highly formulaic Old French epic was
also orally composed. This logically suspect proposition is,
necessarily, a grossly over-simplified summary of their position,
which is supported by secondary considerations; the reader is
referred to the writings of representative scholars for full
expositions: Bowra, *36*, *37*; Duggan, *55*, *57*, *58*; Lord, *104*; Parry
and Lord, *124*; Louis, *105*, *106*; Magoun, *108*; Rychner, *138*, *139*;
cf. also Finnegan, *68* and, for a hostile response, Calin, *47*, *48*).
Traditionalists would generally believe that a poem like the *Roland*
was sung by many different singers over the centuries, each
performer re-creating the poem at each singing, improvising on the
basis of a story-line which could be altered at will, by the use of the
traditional system of formulaic composition. There would be no
fixed form of the poem, only many rival and differing singings, and
our manuscript texts would be accidental recordings in writing
which betray, by their very nature, the genre which they
misleadingly reflect.

   I can only state here that I disagree with this theory as applied
to *Roland* and the other extant *chansons de geste,* and refer readers
to my article, *155*; I have seen nothing since 1969 to make me
retract the conclusions reached there. These are briefly that oral
tradition accounts very well for the transmission of the historical
events which underlie almost every *chanson de geste*, and for the
enormous distortion which characterises that transmission; but that
our written texts are the work of *writing* poets, imitating at first the
oral poems with which they had grown up. This imitation
necessarily involved reproducing the formulaic style of the oral
tradition, but the textual stability of *chansons de geste* preserved in

several manuscripts shows that they already have a fixed written form; the total lack of textual correspondence between recorded singings of epics from the genuinely oral Serbo-Croatian tradition, at any rate where more than one poet's version is involved, is qualitatively different. The *Roland* provides a particularly striking demonstration of the difference: the assonanced version represented by Digby was put into rhyme in a new *Roland rimé*, twice as long, in the late twelfth century, and what is significant is the way in which the detail of the assonanced text consistently shows clearly through the rewriting.

The question is of fundamental importance, for it is the very nature of the work which is at stake. An 'individualist' view such as the one I propound here allows for the composition of a text to the satisfaction of an author who takes responsibility before posterity for what he lets out of his hands. He may revise and rearrange over a long period, but ultimately decides that *this* is what he wants to publish (by whatever means: in the case of the *Roland*, it means handing it over for singing by another – for there is no argument about the fact that these poems were sung – and/or for copying). There is the possibility of judging such a poet's stylistic decisions; in the 'traditionalist' model, there *is* no *Chanson de Roland*; there are only singings, more or less good, of the Roland subject, only the story-line of which has permanent existence. Rudy Spraycar (*145*, p.70) sums it up admirably:

> Unlike the oral poet, who is relatively restricted by the very principle of economy in diction without which he could not compose at all, the literate poet makes deliberate use of a given formula in a particular context. His work can thus admit of a close reading.

It is to such a close reading that we may now turn.

2. Interpretation: the death of Roland

Nominated by a treacherous stepfather to command the rearguard of twenty thousand picked warriors during the withdrawal of his lord, Charlemagne, from Spain, and faced with overwhelming Saracen odds, the emperor's nephew Roland refuses to recall the main army until it is too late for rescue, and dies heroically with all his men. The emperor returns when Roland finally sounds his horn, and avenges the dead by the total defeat of the Saracens and the punishment of the traitor. Such in brief outline is the subject of the *Chanson de Roland*. How are we to understand it? How does the poet see his hero and his actions?

The Digby manuscript has no title: the one which we use here was given by the poem's first editor, Francisque Michel, in 1837. Yet, apart from one major scholar (Pauphilet, *125*, pp.65-89), who argued the case for naming the poem after Charlemagne, no doubt has ever seriously existed about the propriety of Michel's choice. Roland's prestige, his words, decisions and actions dominate the epic until his death, some three-fifths of the way through; but even after this event, the vengeance of the emperor is above all for his nephew, even though its consummation in the Baligant episode (see Chapter 3) has cosmic significance for the struggle between Cross and Crescent. Indeed the sequel valorises the death which is being avenged by placing it causally in the context of the defeat of Islam at the highest level.

Roland is very clearly the hero, whose death – the climax of a glorious disaster, not a defeat – nevertheless occurs in the perspective of the great collective effort of the Christians on what is a Crusade in all but name. Two characteristics of the *chanson de geste*, which differentiate it sharply from the romance, may be commented on in this connection: in the epic, the heroism of the protagonists is always seen and measured against the background of the general, united striving towards an important national or religious goal, whereas romance tends to study the hero and his spiritual development for their own sake.

Connected with this is an evident sense that the epic represents, on a legendary, perhaps almost mythic plane, historical truth for the hearers. Within a century of the composition of the *Roland*, the versatile Arrasian poet Jehan Bodel showed a clear understanding of this difference when, in the preamble to his *Chanson des Saisnes*, he contrasted the 'pleasing vanities' of the romance with the truth, manifested every day, of the *chansons de geste* (*24*, ll.9-11). Hemming persuasively demonstrates this point in his Introduction (*1*, p.xi), referring to one among several known monastic forgeries of charters perpetrated to give material advantage to the monasteries concerned. In this document, from Saint Yrieix (I add to his list, cf. Bédier, *31*, IV, pp.420-24), Charles, Roland, Oliver, Turpin, Guillaume d'Orange ('Curbinaso') and others, some totally fictional, are called upon as 'witnesses'. Hemming remarks: 'It would never have occurred even to the most inept of forgers to seek to authenticate a document by including the names of such heroes of romance as Lancelot, Galahad, Gawain or Tristan'. This encapsulates the point perfectly.

In conformity with this exemplary, historic role, the epic hero is much less subject to character analysis than his romance counterpart. This is emphasised by a number of recent critics (Hunt, *85*, *86*; Kay, *90*; Cook, *50*, pp.xiii-xiv; Short, *9*, pp.19-20; Suard, *148*, pp.42-43). 'S'inscrivant dans le cadre d'un type', writes Suard,

> le personnage épique n'est pas l'objet d'analyses approfondies de la part du narrateur, qui se borne à de courtes indications sur le comportement de ses héros [...] Mais, la plupart du temps, la construction du personnage s'effectue par le moyen des *actes* qu'il accomplit et des paroles qu'il prononce ou que d'autres profèrent à son sujet [...] il est donc aventureux de rechercher dans le héros épique les marques d'un

'caractère' que le poète n'a pas pu ou pas voulu y mettre.

I would certainly agree that this is in general a just description of epic 'characters', and that, as Hunt says, the articulation of the action takes precedence over the analysis of character. The psychological complexity of moments such as the introspective self-criticism of Guillaume in the *Charroi de Nîmes* (*16*, ll.790-804) are rare in their detail and sensitivity; and even this revelation of self-doubt is mediated through dialogue. It is powerfully true that it is by actions and words, rather than authorial/narratorial analysis, that we learn about the thoughts and dispositions of our heroes and come to judge them: the genre is to a considerable extent *dramatic*.

But learn and judge we do, and the best of our poets finally present us with believable, not wholly two-dimensional portraits. The fact that there is little or no analysis does not mean that the psychology of all the *dramatis personae* is non-existent or necessarily rudimentary. Characterisation is a natural concomitant of a well-organised story-line of any complexity, as I have argued elsewhere in relation to the *Roland*: 'Actions, words, choices of lines of conduct are certainly the constituent parts of the tragic subject; but they cannot help being to some extent revelatory of motives and character, as Aristotle himself says in chap. 6 of the *Poetics*' (*162*, p.184). And, in turn, the articulation of the action is in my view based upon, and arises from, the clash of motivations and personalities.

Aristotle brings us to the question, raised in the Foreword, of the interpretation of the poem we are studying: my contention, like that of Hunt (to whose two articles quoted above I was reacting), is that the *Chanson de Roland*, up to the death of the hero, is constructed as a tragedy, though the apotheosis at that moment wrenches the whole work out of the tragic sphere, and brings it closer to the genre of Saints' Lives. If, as Cook warns (*50*, p.xii), such a reading adversely affects the unity of the whole, so be it: the search for 'unity' is of dubious application to mediaeval texts in any case. I shall nevertheless have occasion later to point repeatedly to the hero's continued domination of the poem even after his death.

Neither Hunt nor I suppose any knowledge of Aristotle in the poet: if he appears to construct his tragic action according to the precepts of the Greek philosopher, it must be purely instinctive and explicable by the fact that the *Poetics*, for all the imperfections of the version transmitted to us, do identify the ingredients which give human beings of many times and places the tragic pleasure or *epieikeia* which is the sign that the tragedian has succeeded in his purpose. The dramatic technique of the *Roland*, about 40% of which consists of direct speech, perhaps helps to explain why many readers have felt that cathartic pleasure over this poem, even though it is self-evidently not a play.

It is further my contention that the poet, consciously or unconsciously, founds his tragic action on well-observed traits of character and motivation which ring true today, as in 1100, because they are fundamentally true of human behaviour. While the characterisation of Roland or Ganelon is not wide-ranging or comprehensive – they are not 'rounded characters' by any means – we learn, from their words and deeds, what we need to know about them, and what we learn rings true. (The gulf which separates us from the thought-forms of the twelfth century has perhaps on occasion been exaggerated: see e.g. Crist, *51*, pp.14-15; Robertson, *135*, p.3. The study of literature would be barren indeed if we did not often recognise ourselves and our own contemporaries in the mirror of the more perceptive writings of even our distant ancestors.)

It is certainly true, of course, that it is difficult to be sure that we have indeed understood the intentions of the mediaeval author instead of reading into what he writes our own ideas and suppositions. I have therefore attempted, in recent work, to enlist in this enterprise the very structure of the narrative (*162, 165, 166*), and I believe that one can sometimes argue from the way the poet organises his material to what he wishes his listeners to understand.

This approach will be employed where appropriate in the close reading which follows below; like Cook (*50*, p.xiv) I cannot see a better arrangement of the material, for my purposes, than a full-length interpretative commentary. Not everything can be commented on, of course, for reasons of space, and I shall necessarily stress those elements which seem to me significant in the perspective of my interpretation of the poem; but I hope that I shall not fail to face up to lines which do not fit in with my view; I shall also comment on matters which readers may find useful in the general aim of understanding and appreciating the text. Matters of poetic technique will be dealt with in a separate chapter later.

Before beginning this commentary, I must draw attention to contrary points of view to my own, so as to be able to concentrate on my exegesis without continual polemical excursions, though I shall refer to opposing arguments on specific points where it is necessary.

I shall in the first place be courting controversy by stressing what appears to me to be Roland's tragic fault: his *desmesure*, taking as my starting-point a very clear formulation by Gaston Paris: '[Le désastre de Roncevaux] provient en grande mesure de la faute du héros, de sa *desmesure*, comme on disait en ancien français, d'un mot qui rend parfaitement l'idée de l'*hubris* homérique [. . .]' (*122*, p.75). I am thus, as part of my deliberately reactionary exegesis, seeking to re-examine, restate and perhaps amplify the case for a view once widespread among specialists, but today considered by many scholars to be out of date (I draw this conclusion from much published work, but also from private conversations with colleagues). In some cases, such as the articles by Tony Hunt which I have been referring to, and the introduction to Ian Short's edition (*9*, p.20), the word *desmesure* is now considered irrelevant to the debate ('le débat stérile sur la prétendue "démesure" de Roland' is Short's expression). Hunt, expounding what he rightly sees as the tragic action leading to the hero's death, is however not convinced of the need for Roland's *hamartia* or tragic error to have a moral dimension: a simple mistake suffices to launch tragedy (*85*, p.4 *et passim*).

Here I would make one preliminary point, in awareness particularly of the danger of anachronism (cf. Crist, *51*, pp.10-11). Old French literature, in spite of the Christian beliefs of the society from which it springs, does have a taste for tragedy, as the Tristan story shows. There are *chansons de geste* which either are tragic (*Raoul de Cambrai*) or come very close to it, the hero's sudden conversion being necessary to prevent a tragic outcome (*Girart de Roussillon, La Chevalerie Ogier*). Further, the word *desmesure* is explicitly used of Raoul de Cambrai (*23*, line 320; cf. Owen, *120*) and, if they do not use the word, other poets clearly make Girart de Roussillon, Ogier le Danois and Charlemagne himself guilty of it in, respectively, the epics of revolt mentioned and in *Renaut de Montauban*. The word is used too by non-epic writers like Marie de France, who illuminatingly discusses what she clearly sees as a fatal flaw in her character Equitan (*22*, *Equitan*, ll.17-20), though in his case the lack of measure relates to his love affair with a vassal's wife and to its tragic outcome (cf. *Yonec*, ll.201-10). Modern critics have had no difficulties with these interpretations. There is therefore no reason in principle for excluding the possibility of such an exegesis in the case of Roland: the word *desmesure* does not appear in our poem, but he is accused of lacking *mesure* at line 1725 by Oliver. We shall have to interpret this line, in its context, in due course.

The rest of the paragraph in Short's edition referred to above suggests that he leans towards one of two schools of thought which I identified in my contribution to the Aix-en-Provence Congress of the Société Rencesvals in 1973 (*157*). These 'schools' (and I recognise that there is some over-simplification in the use of the term) have in common, though for opposite reasons, the proposition that Roland has no moral fault of any sort, and is an exemplary figure. In Aristotelian terms, at any rate, such a hero is incompatible with the 'man of middling virtue' who is the only suitable tragic hero, since a totally virtuous man's passage from prosperity to adversity is shocking rather than productive of fear and pity. In this sense, therefore, the whole notion of the tragic nature of Roland's death is ruled out in such interpretations.

This is especially true of the view that Roland is from the start a saintly imitator of Christ, a *christomimetes*, who is right when everyone else, and especially Oliver, is wrong, and who knowingly sacrifices his rearguard and himself in order to ensure that Charlemagne brings the conquest of Spain for God to a proper conclusion. Such a Roland can certainly not be said to pass from prosperity to adversity: his apotheosis must, on this interpretation, be his just and joyous reward.

This 'school' was I think inspired by a short but extremely influential article published in 1957 by Alfred Foulet: 'Is Roland Guilty of *desmesure*?' (*70*), and by the section on *Roland* in Robertson's *Preface to Chaucer* (*135*, pp.162-71). Foulet seems to have influenced many scholars by his analysis, according to which Roland knows that 'a terrible sacrifice is demanded of him [...] Only by dying and sending others to their death can he bring about the triumph of the cause he champions' (p.148). This 'dark truth' cannot be communicated to others, not even Oliver. Such an interpretation obviously sees Roland as motivated above all by his commitment to the Faith, and the logical development of Foulet's note came in a spate of articles and books (like Robertson's) in which Roland is seen as the flawless Christian hero *par excellence*. These influences can I believe be seen in the evolution in the thinking of the late Pierre Le Gentil, who is still speaking clearly about the hero's '*démesure*' in the first edition of his well-known book on the poem (1955, pp.102, 124ff.), but this is somewhat attenuated in the second edition (*101*, pp.123-32, esp.127), and even more so in his article of 1968 (*102*).

In my 1973 paper, I referred to and discussed Le Gentil's evolving interpretation in the context of other publications, then relatively recent, which took this line. It must suffice for present purposes if I refer readers to that paper for the details. It was later reprinted in *Olifant* 1, 1974 (*157*, pp.21-47), preceded by an excellent example of the line of argument I have been summarising, an article by Larry S. Crist (*51*). Roland is inspired by the Folly of the Cross, which is wiser than the wisdom of men (I Corinthians 1, 18-25 [not II Corinthians, as stated]). Crist, warning against anachronistic exegesis, goes on to argue (following the general lines of Foulet's article) that the only appropriate level on which to interpret the *Roland* is that of allegory, an allegory of the Christian life (pp.15-20) with the eponymous hero as the type of the saint, the *imitator Christi* who accepts death cheerfully, for he has already defeated it.

Since these publications, the 'school' which sees Roland as a hero inspired by Christian enthusiasm and fundamentally right against all those who oppose him has produced a number of major works and articles, some of which I list here, so that readers can follow up this line of thinking: Brault (*7*; *41*); Goldin (*13*, Introduction); Pensom (*127*); Hecht (*77*); Uitti (*150*, Chap. II); Short (*9*, Introduction); Hemming, *1*, Introduction).

The other grouping referred to in *157* is what might be called the 'feudal school', which had and I think has rather fewer members. The founding text here may have been George Fenwick Jones's *The Ethos of the Song of Roland* (*88*). Jones, after a study of the words in *Roland* which have a moral meaning (a study which is deeply flawed because it restricts itself solipsistically to the poem under examination), compares its ethical and social structures with those of the Germanic tribes. For this scholar, Roland's rashness in refusing to sound the horn would, in the 'shame culture' which Jones sees as the social context, be blameworthy only if it led to a defeat, which it does not. Scholars who take a somewhat similar line, such as D.D.R. Owen (*118, 119, 120*), Normand R. Cartier (*49*), William W. Kibler (*95, 96*), tend to see Roland as the perfect feudal vassal, dying for his lord in an exemplary way. In Jones and Owen, in particular, the Christian element is seen as minimal, a veneer covering a poem basically Germanic and pagan in its assumptions and its ethos.

An important recent work which must be placed in this current of thought, though, unlike Jones, it does not seek to go back to the German tribes of Tacitus, is Robert F. Cook's *The Sense of the 'Song of Roland'* (*50*). Here, in a very consistent close reading (which does however at times ignore the lines which do not fit), Roland is presented in a primarily feudal light, as the vassal who carries out his duties and keeps precisely the promises made to his lord. The turning point for Cook is not the first horn scene, but rather the nomination of Roland to the rearguard: the hero makes

certain promises, and the rest of his story shows how he keeps them
to the letter. There is much that is helpful in this work, but the
problem for me is precisely that one has to look at Roland's words
as though one were a lawyer scrutinising a contract. Is that the spirit
of epic?

Readers will make of these works (as of the present
monograph) what they will, and it would be pointless to· try to
summarise further. I must refer to my 1973 article (*157*) for my
reactions to these views, for I would still endorse what I wrote on
these matters then. One noteworthy feature which almost all the
works cited have in common is that, in order to present Roland as
perfect (either as exemplary Christian martyr or as exemplary feudal
warrior with little or no Christian dimension), critics attack Oliver
for moral blindness (much is made of his loss of vision at his death)
and even for an unwillingness to die which borders, according to
some, on cowardice. Furthermore, Charlemagne, Naimon and the
French have to be represented as easily duped, as over-eager to
accept a way out of finishing the campaign by military means
because they are battle-weary and long for home. The interpretative
commentary, which now follows, will have to see how far such
claims can be substantiated from the text. I acknowledge in advance
that I am putting the case for one interpretation; it has to be
remembered that the dramatic technique of the poet avoids authorial
judgements, leaving interpretation to us. In that sense the work may
be called ambiguous (cf. Vinaver, *168*); it has certainly given rise to
several, mutually contradictory, exegeses. But I doubt whether the
poet *meant* his poem to be ambiguous, and my purpose is to see how
far the characters' words and behaviour, and the very structure of
the text, guide us in the task of understanding his conception of the
subject.

INTERPRETATIVE COMMENTARY

Laisse I

A masterly exposition: in nine lines we learn that
Charlemagne and his army have been seven years in Spain, that

nothing remains to be conquered but Saragossa, ruled over by the pagan king Marsile, who has no hope of avoiding disaster. There are inaccuracies of fact: the picture of Islam, in which there are said to be several gods, of whom one is Mahomet (we here have two names out of four or five common ones which tend to be permutated in 'trinitarian' groups of three, cf. ll. 2580-91, 2696-97, 3490-91) is of course a gross libel on that religion, part of the shameful, lying propaganda which circulated freely in Christian countries at the time of the Crusades, and is repeated in many *chansons de geste*. Saragossa is not on a mountain, but the overtones of the word, coupled with the pregnant word *altaigne* in line 3 ('high' in the physical sense, pre-echoing the mountain in line 6, but also 'haughty') add prestige to the land conquered and to be conquered. But mediaeval ears would also have picked up something else, of importance to our theme: seven years is a very long time for a feudal army to remain in the field: the Saracen plan will depend upon the implications of this (laisse IV, etc., see below). The last line ends with the mysterious siglum AOI, which recurs frequently, normally at the end of a laisse. Its meaning has not been satisfactorily resolved (*1*, n.9), but it may be considered as a sort of refrain.

Laisse II

Serves above all to repeat the point that, militarily, the Saracens have no hope (repetition and echo are very important devices in *Roland*, for both narrative and stylistic reasons). Marsile calls a council exactly as a French feudal lord would (there is little attempt at local colour in the poem), stating baldly that the whole Saracen army cannot hope to stand up to the Christian one (ll.16-19, cf. ll.564-69). This is one of the given facts of the story, and it is important for our assessment of Roland's later decision not to call the army back. At line 16, France has its standing epithet of *dulce*, even in Marsile's mouth; note also the overtones of the name *Blanc*andrin the wise (cf. line 24) counsellor, implying white hair, and *Valfunde*, 'Valley of the depths, shadows'(?); all but one of the toponyms beginning *Val* are applied to pagans (I use this latter term reluctantly, very loosely as does the poet, to avoid repetition).

Laisses III-IV

Blancandrin's plan, revealed gradually. Praise is given (ll.24-26) to his vassalic qualities and wisdom (such recognition of qualities in pagans is not uncommon, and makes them more impressive adversaries). The initially surprising advice to send tribute to Charles, with a promise of conversion and vassaldom, all guaranteed by their own sons as hostages, is revealed in IV to be a desperate, though calculated, means of escape. It sounds like surrender, with tribute as an earnest of it and cast-iron guarantees (given the great importance attached to heirs in mediaeval society); it is cold-blooded but effective deception. The Frankish army, once home, will break up like the *ost banie* it is (ll.211, 1469, cf. Cook, *50*, p.6, though ll.34, 133 show the presence of mercenaries too), and, after seven years' service, will be impossible to reassemble. At the price of their sons' lives, the Saracens will be safe.

Laisses V-VII

The sending of the message. There is some attempt at mild exoticism in the names of the pagan messengers (cf. perhaps too a trace of local colour in 'bright Spain', *clere Espagne la bele*, line 59, as compared with *dulce France*?). Later poets will develop lists like those at ll.63-67 in the direction of the grotesque, though note already here a sinister paradox in *Malbien*, line 67. The classical symbolism of olive branches, which implies clerical education in the author, is explained, and the message is restated, with a sort of religious blackmail at line 82 and a repetition of the clinching point, the hostages, at line 87. The rich trappings of the white mules promise much by implication, but are also part of normal epic idealisation (cf. *1*, n.109). The last line, 95, echoes the last of laisse I in its first hemistich, to accentuate the inevitability of Charles's being deceived. Yet the Saracen offer is such, and has such a guarantee, that the deception will not make Charles look foolish or over-eager.

Laisse VIII

A picture of an army in a high state of morale. Those who see the Frankish army as battle-weary and ready to jump at any offer to go home must explain away this laisse, which stresses the most recent victory won and the booty distributed (ll.97-100), and shows the army relaxing with games or practising its military skills (ll.110-13). There is a suggestion earlier, at ll.35-36, to be echoed at ll.135-36, that it is time for Charles to return to Aix, but this is part of the Saracens' plea, and is not taken up by any Christian, not even Ganelon. Turpin does later refer to the Franks' labours over seven years (line 267), but this seems merely a specious, slightly jocular argument in support of his desire to volunteer for the mission to Marsile: it is palpably at odds with the actual behaviour of the Franks in laisse VIII. This ends with a grandiose picture of Charlemagne on a golden throne in the shade (on this *locus amoenus* topos, see Chapter 4, p.120), white-haired, handsome and proud in bearing, climaxing in the memorable epitome of line 119.

Laisses IX-XI

The message is stated before the French, preceded by a greeting tactfully couched in the name of the Christian God (contrast in different ways ll.416-17 and 428-29), as an earnest of conversion. The stress in IX is on the tribute, with no mention of the hostages. This is deliberate: after silently invoking God (line 137) and bowing his head in thought, Charles is thus made quite naturally to ask about guarantees (ll.143-46). This is dramatic technique (cf. pp.15-16 above) at work in practice, bringing out an important point, the number and importance of the hostages (ll.147-50), by question and answer. The promise to follow and be baptised, adumbrated in one line at 136, is also expanded (ll.151-55) – a form of incremental repetition very dear to this author. All this is intercalated between two reactions of Charles: ll.139-42 characteristically pick up and develop the end of the previous laisse, and stress the wisdom of this king, who always speaks after reflection. The development includes the reversal of *baisset sun chef* (line 138) by *se redrecet* (line 142), and the fact that now his face is haughty: his question is a challenging one. On the other hand, the stress on Marsile's desire for baptism produces a different reaction: Charlemagne's first thought, line 156, is for the Saracen's salvation, and this marks the pressure on a Christian monarch, who is after all in Spain to convert the infidel, to listen seriously to a plea such as Blancandrin's. There is no doubt of the religious motivation of Charles throughout (cf. ll.164, 670). Laisse XI, in addition to details of hospitality offered to the messengers, adds another touch, typically in the lapidary final line, 167: though clearly a theocratic ruler, with a direct responsibility to God, he is also idealised (from a baronial point of view) as a feudal monarch who listens to and acts on the advice of his vassals, something he has *willed* (*voelt il*) to do. (For the background to this ideal synthesis of theocratic and feudal monarchy, see Ullmann, *151*, Part II.)

Laisse XII

Picking up ll.166-67, this laisse shows some of the major barons assembling for Charlemagne's council (some well known from later epics, others episodic). The list climaxes with Roland and Oliver and, last of all, the traitor Ganelon (line 178; cf. *1*, n.177 on the Judas-overtone here, but add Matthew 10. 4). The order allows the poet to emphasise the treason which was clearly known to the hearers ('*la* traïsun'). There is no effort to create suspense: it is a well-known story, the inevitability of whose outcome adds to the tragic dimension of this part of the poem (line 179; cf. Goldin, *13*, pp.12-18).

Ganelon's role is structurally very important: at this stage there is nothing to connect Roland with the Saracens, who want only to ensure that Charlemagne and his army leave Spain. The quarrel and Ganelon's consequent desire for vengeance, coinciding with his role as emissary, make the link: the Saracens are persuaded by Ganelon that Roland is the obstacle to the success of their plan and that they must eliminate him.

Laisses XIII-XVI

The first phase of the council debates the desirability of entering into discussions with the Saracens. Charles repeats the message, without referring to the hostages, though we are clearly expected to understand that the terms are public (cf. line 241). He makes no recommendation, but *mais* (line 191) implies caution. The French echo this except for Roland, who does not approve the emperor's words and rises to 'speak against him' (ll.194-95; *li, pace* Cook, *50*, p.10, is personal). As Charles has made no proposition, the use of *cuntredire* is significant: Roland objects to the matter even being discussed, and his first words are characteristically uncompromising: he characterises himself by them. Evoking his own record of conquest in the last seven years – primarily a way of establishing his right to be heard rather than a sign of pride, perhaps, but showing him at once as very confident of his own worth – he reminds his hearers (and tells us) that Marsile has offered precisely such terms before (apparently without hostages, if this means the message as repeated by Charles) and then treacherously beheaded Basin and Basile, sent to discuss them. He ascribes this disaster to rash advice given by the council at that time and reminds Charles of his duty to avenge his men, demanding that the war be finished as it was started, with the utmost energy. Brault (*7*, p.133), reads war-weariness into the earlier advice given by the French, but there is no hint of it in the text.

The emperor does not respond, and the French are silent except for Ganelon who, in lines which parallel and echo Roland's intervention (compare ll.195-96 with ll.218, 220), cuttingly rejects Roland's advice. *Ja mar* (literally 'Indeed in an evil hour') before a verb in the future constitutes an energetic negative imperative: where Roland had urged Charles 'Never trust Marsile', Ganelon now echoes his words with 'Never trust a fool', clearly stigmatising Roland with the epithet. Brault (*7*, p.133) and Hunt (*85*, pp.4-8) both see the hostility between the men as arising only during this scene, Ganelon taking Roland's reference to *legerie* personally. I agree with those, among them Hemming (*1*, n.220ff.), who believe that the poet, relying on the audience's knowledge of the subject, implies previous dislike based partly on the step-relationship (line 277; cf. van Emden *162*, pp.186-87). The poet, masterfully, never allows Ganelon to explain his hatred precisely, but gives him, much later (line 3758), a cryptic reference to some quarrel over possessions as his reason. In my view, this vagueness is deliberate and the mark of genius, just as Shakespeare never gives a clear reason for Iago's hatred of Othello.

Ganelon's argument, shorn of the snide attacks on Roland, is apparently reasonable: Marsile is conceding what the campaign is all about: he will hold Spain as Charles's vassal and become a Christian. It is wrong, he says, to reject such a plea out of hand; but then he returns to the personal attack on Roland, whose counsel is made from foolishness (line 229) and pride, *orguill* (line 228). On this latter word, which only Ganelon ever (but several times) applies to Roland, and which is certainly highly pejorative, see Kibler (*95*, pp.147-60). I agree that, unlike say Girart de Roussillon, Roland has not the extreme, damnable form of pride concerned; but that does not exclude the possibility of his pushing 'legitimate pride – the pride of a dauntless warrior', in Kibler's words, to the point of *desmesure* (cf. Renoir, *133*, p.577).

That Ganelon's attitude is on the face of it reasonable (were it not insincere, see below) is suggested by laisse XVI, in which Naimon restates the argument without the personal attacks, and endorses it, bringing in the hostages (line 241) as the clinching point. Naimon is praised in high terms by the author (line 231, cf. line 775) and he seems to be the Nestor of the army. He is certainly given this role in all later *chansons de geste*, and, in spite of some suggestions (e.g. Pensom, *127*, pp.88-89) to the contrary, there is nothing in *Roland* to imply that the tradition of his wisdom is not yet established (cf. *saives hom*, line 248; for a contrary view on the adjective, see Misrahi and Hendrickson, *112*, pp.366-67; *113*, pp.229-30; cf. Venckeleer, *167*, pp.457-65; Hunt, *87*, p.203). He always acts as Charlemagne's close counsellor, repeatedly stepping in to bring the king to a necessary decision (ll.774-82, 831-32, 1790-95, 2423-28). The French agree with him (line 243).

Laisses XVII-XXVI

The nomination of Ganelon. That Charles asks for nominations for the dangerous mission without further ado at line 244 shows the working of his council. We have seen that it is Charlemagne's will to rule through the agreement of his vassals (line 167). Throughout, even when he thoroughly disagrees (ll.3793-814), the emperor does not override the collective counsel of his men, though, as we shall see, he reserves the right to veto something before judgement has been given. (For a concise analogy in modern terms, see Cook, *50*, p.17.)

What happens now is highly significant, the ordering of the episode showing the author carefully steering the reactions of the audience. He has Naimon volunteer first, even before Roland. Why? I have argued elsewhere at some length (*162*, pp.186-92; cf. Short, *9*, n.245) that the poet wishes to draw our attention to the silence of Ganelon (cf. Picherit, *129*; Faral, *67*, p.67). He, after all, had vehemently proposed the mission; his silence, emphasised by the volunteering of the 'seconder of the motion', shows that his proposition is intended to be seen as having nothing to do with any desire for peace or mercy on the defeated enemy, but simply as motivated by hostility to Roland personally, to humiliate him. This is substantiated later by the splendidly illogical self-pity of ll.310-11, but here Ganelon's silence is made significant by the very disposition of the text, and it is consequently possible to argue that, in these circumstances, Roland's coming nomination of his stepfather is not neutral, but aggressive. It follows that his *hamartia* is not morally neutral, and that Roland should at least have been able to foresee Ganelon's reaction (see van Emden, *162*, p.182 and n.2).

Charlemagne's tone to Naimon is brusque (line 215), although he gives his reason for refusing: Naimon's wisdom, which is indispensable (ll.248-50). The emperor clearly keeps a power of veto, in spite of his decision to act in all things through the consent of his vassals (line 167). He considers Naimon too precious to expose to such a mission, and his embarrassment expresses itself in brusqueness.

At once Roland proposes himself – already, we feel no surprise at his irrepressibility – but he is at once opposed by Oliver, who, from his knowledge of his friend, gives reasons which, once again, do not surprise us (ll.256-57). Roland's uncompromising and bellicose nature is brought out by dramatic means: opposition from his comrade. Oliver, it should be remembered, is completely without historical basis: with his Latin-based name (he is the only Christian without a Germanic one) associated biblically and classically with wisdom (Brault, 7, pp.12, 69), he has obviously been created (though in a version earlier than Digby) to act as a foil to Roland. Both self-nominations are, again brusquely, vetoed by Charles, who adds that none of the Twelve Peers, the elite group of comrades-in-arms led by Roland and Oliver, is to go.

A final attempt at self-nomination comes from Turpin, not one of the Peers in this version, but a very important member of the army: the Archbishop of Rheims, whose prowess with sword and lance give him great prestige, rather than his clerical status (cf. ll.1508-09, 2242-44). Again, he is irritably (*par maltalent*, line 271) vetoed. The self-nominations, led by Naimon, and resulting in a total of fourteen barons being prevented from going as being too valuable to send, not only underscore Ganelon's failure to volunteer, they also produce a situation in which the nomination of Ganelon by Roland (line 277) cannot be a neutral act (as I have suggested above, p.29, against the opinion of Cook, 50, p.23). The endorsement by the French, hitherto forestalled each time by Charlemagne's veto, stresses the fact that Ganelon, though wise enough (line 279) to act as ambassador, is not *too* valuable to be sent.

These factors, added to the realisation that the hated stepson, a younger and more distinguished man, has in effect used the authority of the emperor and the assent of the French to force Ganelon to the logical end of his own proposition, are enough to make the latter react with uncontrolled anger (ll.280-91). It is a reaction which rings completely true psychologically, as anyone will know who has ever as a child been bested by a younger and apparently favoured sibling using parental authority to impose his or her will, or, as an adult, lost an important issue at a meeting through the intervention of a junior colleague.

The immediacy of this outburst is unique to *O*, other witnesses having a different order here (see the alternative line numbers in the Hemming/Whitehead edition and some others). In the alternative version, Whitehead's laisses XXIV and XXIII, in that order, follow line 279, with ll.280-309 coming only then. This makes Ganelon reach the point of defying Roland, Oliver and the Peers at once, and

defers the unfocused mouthing in Whitehead (ll.286-91), together
with Roland's contemptuous reply (echoing Ganelon's own sneers
at ll.228-29) and subsequent laughter (or sarcastic smile?), which in
O work to increase Ganelon's wrath, to the end of the process. It
does have the minor advantage of justifying literally Ganelon's
assertion that Charlemagne is ordering him to carry out this act of
service (line 298) – Charles does not intervene formally until
line 317 in *O* – but the emperor's silence at Ganelon's nomination
is an endorsement in itself. The loss of gradation in the latter's
anger, which in *O* climaxes in the *desfi* and the immediately
following insolent retort to the emperor himself, pointing out the
latter's inability to protect his emissaries (ll.329-30), is enough to
entitle one to prefer *O* here, as so often elsewhere, over the other
versions.

Taking *O*'s order as being likely to represent what the author
wanted, we see Ganelon's reaction characteristically gaining in
precision with repetition (see Chapter 4, pp.112-13 below). From
the unfocused threat of ll.289-91, we pass to the linking of the
promised vengeance with the mission at ll.299-301, through the
statement of hatred which follows Roland's scorn (ll.302-07) and
the turning to Charles with self-pitying acceptance of the mission
(ll.308-16), to the exaggerated, almost paranoid, statement that
Roland is the real author of all this (line 322, cf. line 321 and Cook,
50, p.25), and so to the *desfi* (ll.323-26). Ganelon calls on Charles
to witness it, and he will later point to this moment as a defence
against the charge of treason (ll.3775-79, where we will examine
the argument's validity). For the moment, let us note the impeccable
control with which the author, at least in *O*'s version, has made the
scene escalate to the crucial climax of the challenge.

In the scene just analysed, Roland's part has not been
inconsiderable: after the nomination itself (well merited, but bound
to infuriate Ganelon), Roland does nothing to reduce the tension,
answering anger with contempt (the offer to go in his stepfather's
place is insulting for the reasons given at ll.296-97) and then
mocking Ganelon's threats. The latter certainly loses control, but
Roland's stoking of the fire is to be noted.

Laisses XXV-XXVII

Ganelon's unwilling (line 332) acceptance of the insignia of office is accompanied by a bad omen, the dropping of the glove. Roland will remind him of this in a further contemptuous exchange later (ll.763-65), during the parallel scene in which Ganelon nominates him to the rearguard; but the immediate effect is to increase the tragic inevitability the audience feels. This is increased by Ganelon's rejoinder (line 336) and by the forebodings of laisse XXVII. Between these two moments, we note an astonishing manifestation of Charlemagne's immense prestige: he makes the sign of the Cross over his vassal and absolves him, an assumption of priestly powers which exceeds even the myth which formed around him (Bender, *33*, pp.9-26), and is is quite unparalleled in history, in spite of some theorising on the status of the anointed king (see e.g. Kern, *94*, pp.71-76). Charles, in this idealised conception, becomes a Priest-King like Melchisedech (Genesis 14. 18-20, cf. Hebrews 7. 1-21), an Old Testament figure who was himself a 'type' of Christ in typological thought. (On the mediaeval legend of Charlemagne, see also Folz, *69*.)

Laisse XXVII increases the foreboding through the careful arming of Ganelon (ll.342-48) and the lamentations of the knights of his household (ll.349-52). The reference to his high reputation is not to be discounted: the poet has already (ll.280-85) shown us the future traitor as a splendid figure, imposing and handsome in his anger (cf. de Riquer, *134*, pp.96-98). This, in the words of a later epic poet, Bertrand de Bar-sur-Aube (*20*, ll.27-45), is a great lord of high reputation who falls like Lucifer through pride and envy, an analysis with which we may well agree at this point. The potentially disastrous effects of the quarrel for the state are stressed by ll.353-56, a menacing promise to resort to clan vendetta against Roland, should Ganelon be killed. Charlemagne himself will be unable to protect his nephew (ll.353-54). (The horrors of such spiralling vengeance are well painted in *Raoul de Cambrai*, a later epic of which earlier versions will certainly have been extant.) Then the laisse turns to pathos with Ganelon's refusal to let others die with him and his instructions about the succession to his lands. Like ll.310-17 and ll.329-30, however, ll.358-64 continue to underline the hollowness of his original proposal.

Laisses XXVIII-XXXI

Picking up and developing, again in a characteristic way, the last line of laisse XXVII, the poet describes Ganelon riding towards Saragossa: in three menacing lines (ll.367-69) he shows Ganelon, in an olive-grove, catching up with Blancandrin, but only because the latter has deliberately slackened his pace, and the two then speaking 'with great wisdom' (echoing the symbolism of the olive trees) to each other. (I disagree with the attempt of Misrahi and Hendrickson (*112*, pp.366-67, *113*, pp.229-30) to depreciate *saveir* and its cognates as being found in 'bad company' like Blancandrin, and so meaning mere 'cleverness'. A good quality may be put to evil use, and is all the more sinister for it.) The Saracen, who (religion aside) has also been admired by the poet (ll.24-26), and whose chief quality is such wisdom turned to evil ends, diplomatically sounds out his companion, praising Charles and asking what his purposes are. Ganelon replies with non-committal praise (ll.375-76).

Blancandrin begins laisse XXIX taking his previous comments an exploratory step further: the French monarch is badly advised by the 'hawks' in his army (ll.378-80). One must never speculate on a fictional situation as if it were reality, but one may say that Blancandrin speaks like one who has caught echoes of the dissensions in the French council. At any rate, Ganelon rises to the bait. He points with undisguised hatred to Roland as the 'hawk' among the Franks, as witness the manner of his triumphant return from a foray near Carcassonne (ll.382-88). We are not, I think, to disbelieve the facts recounted; but it is the interpretation which is significant for Ganelon's biased view: in language which is deeply biblically symbolic, the stepfather sees the stepson as the Tempter himself: the apple recalls Genesis 3, while the reference to the crowns of all kings echoes the third temptation of Christ in Matthew 4. 8-9 (cf. Luke 4. 5-7; see also Brault, *7*, pp.141-43; cf. a different, speculative interpretation, which may be seen as complementary rather than contradictory to the above, in Tony Hunt, *87*). The end of the laisse (ll.389-91) takes up again the wish expressed at line

382, but expresses it in biblical terms: he hopes to see the 'Tempter' fall through his pride (as in the traditional belief about the fall of Lucifer). The last line, which persuasively includes Blancandrin in the first person plural *avriumes*, reinforces the diagnosis: kill Roland, and peace will come.

That Ganelon should accuse Roland of *orgoil*, the most extreme form of pride, here, as often, a stronger word than its modern descendant (see Gougenheim, *74*; cf. Burgess, *45*, pp.103-08), is a biased and unreliable judgement, however much Ganelon's later plan depends on accurate knowledge of his stepson (cf. Kibler, *95*); but one may well, with de Riquer (*134*, p.95), see in it a certain youthful vainglory. There are degrees of pride (Le Gentil, *101*, pp.124-25).

In laisse XXX, question and answer elicit further information about Roland: his powerbase is the French within the army, who will follow him anywhere because of his generosity with booty (ll.397-99, cf. line 1167; on line 400, see Hemming note). The laisse adds little to the reasons for doing away with Roland, but increases our feeling that he is indeed a charismatic leader; in the last line Ganelon returns to and confirms Blancandrin's opening comment that there is no foreseeable limit to Roland's conquests. The next laisse follows logically: the two men agree solemnly to seek Roland's death. Le Gentil excellently expresses the nature of Ganelon's crime, which is rooted in a failure to understand the distinction between private vengeance and the great cause which both he and Roland serve (*101*, p.100):

> Ni l'un ni l'autre des interlocuteurs ne songe un seul instant à évoquer le véritable caractère de cette lutte qui oppose deux religions, et cette inconscience achève d'égarer Ganelon sur la véritable portée du pacte, non plus de vengeance mais de trahison désormais, qu'il vient de conclure.

The envoys' arrival in the luxurious setting (ll.406-09) in which Marsile's throne is placed occurs in the midst of an expectant silence, tensely described (ll.411-13).

Laisses XXXII-XXXVIII

The first phase of the discussions leading to Ganelon's formal agreement to commit treason holds surprises. In laisse XXXII, Blancandrin simply introduces Ganelon as Charlemagne's emissary, holding him by the hand (line 415), a normal social convention in the twelfth century, but one which implies an understanding has been reached (Brault, 7, p.146). His summary of his own mission is unremarkable, but we note that he reverts to saluting Marsile in the name of the Saracen 'gods', whereas he had tactfully saluted Charles in that of the Christian God. But Ganelon, after much careful thought and 'with great wisdom' and eloquence (ll.425-27), seems to reject such an approach. In his mouth of course the Christian salutation is a provocation, and the tenor of the message as he gives it orally (ll.430-37) is equally surprising. Given the past record of Marsile, such behaviour is unexpected indeed, particularly since Ganelon is not a negotiator, but simply the bearer of a letter (cf. Cook, 50, pp.30-31).

We have to remember that Ganelon (and this is also his *structural* role) needs to focus the anger and fear of the Saracens upon Roland in order to persuade them to take up arms at all, for Blancandrin's plan had no place for any attack; quite the contrary! In pursuit of his objective, Ganelon has to rouse these emotions, and this means placing himself at no inconsiderable risk. So his version of the message, very different from Charlemagne's summary (laisse XIII) and from his letter (laisse XXXVII), reduces the future fief of Marsile to *half* of Spain and dwells on the humiliating treatment and death which will follow any refusal.

Predictably, Marsile reacts with violence, repeated across the laisse-boundary (ll.438-42): he has to be restrained from striking Ganelon with a javelin. If we had any suspicion that the latter's anger at his nomination was due to cowardice, his behaviour before Marsile is surely enough to dispel it: we have a truly epic glimpse of him partly drawing his sword and addressing a defiant farewell to it, such as heroes make at the height of battle (cf. ll.1464-66) or at the point of death (ll.2304-11). The Saracens intervene, again across the laisse-boundary, with ll.451-55 developing line 450, and Ganelon's defiance is further stressed in heroic terms as he reaffirms his determination to give his message. In ll.460-61, the repetition of *li mandet, par mei li mandet* serves to increase the personal intensity of the expression, while the contrast of *li reis poëstifs* and *son mortel enemi* at the assonance emphasises Marsile's hopeless situation. Throwing off a precious mantle (ll.462-64) is a common sign of angry defiance (cf. ll.281-82) in *chansons de geste*; Ganelon's refusal to let go his sword echoes it, while standing in brilliant stylistic contrast (antithesis ll.464-65) to it. Even the Saracens express admiration (line 467).

With deliberate irony, Ganelon prefaces his repetition of his version of Charlemagne's message with 'A tort vos curuciez' (line 469), as though reassuring words were to follow. He then restates the terms, and, very typically, the poet makes him increase the detail, not only in the humiliations threatened in case of refusal (ll.475-82) but, more significantly, in the naming of Roland as the co-ruler, full of pride, who is to have the other half of Spain (ll.472-74). Only after this threat does he hand over the letter.

Marsile's combination of anger with anxiety to read is beautifully caught in the detail that he throws the broken sealing wax away (line 486). When he reads out the missive, it is apparent that Charles has not used threats like Ganelon, but that he has concentrated, necessarily (cf. Roland at ll.207-13), on vengeance for his murdered vassals Basin and Basile. As Cook (*50*, pp.32-33) rightly points out, Charles will not allow a bond between himself and Marsile (*amer*, line 494, has this meaning) unless he receives cast-iron guarantees this time: the Caliph (*algalife*), Marsile's uncle, must be among the hostages. It is a hard demand, but the business-like rationality of it contrasts with Ganelon's previous threats. It is this contrast that makes Marsile's son ask for orders to kill the emissary (Cook, *50*, p.33; for a different interpretation, see J. Reed, *132*, pp.3-7). Such treacherous violence against an emissary discredits any court at which the idea is entertained, but it leads to another epic moment as Ganelon draws his sword fully and puts his back to a tree as he awaits the fatal onslaught.

Laisses XXXVIII-XLVII

The attack does not come, because the Saracens, including Blancandrin, draw Marsile away to apprise him fully of the situation. Again holding Ganelon by the hand (cf. line 415), Blancandrin brings Ganelon into the *verger* to plan the treason, the wickedness of which is stressed in the last line of laisse XXXVIII. The next stanza briefly shows Marsile apologising for his anger, and offering a gift of furs with golden fastenings; accepting, Ganelon commits himself further. Brault (7, p.135, cf. pp.100-02, 133) considers the 'mainspring' of the traitor's conduct to be avarice; this of course tends to remove responsibility for the quarrel from Roland, and to cast the latter as Christ to Ganelon's Judas. While there is indeed a materialistic streak in the portrayal of Ganelon (ll.518-19, 617-41, 3758, cf. line 3756), and the poet may well want us to feel obscurely that a past quarrel over property partly explains the mutual detestation between him and Roland, Brault's analysis underestimates the passions unleashed at the nomination, which are clearly the 'mainspring' of Ganelon's subsequent actions.

The next three laisses are the first examples of the *laisse similaire* technique, which will be analysed stylistically in the final chapter (pp.113-117; cf. Rychner, *138*, pp.93-95). The same narrative material (often, as here, in dramatic form) is repeated on (usually) three different assonances, both in order to heighten the lyrical intensity of the poem and to dwell on important points. Here Marsile enquires three times, in almost identical terms, how long the aged Charlemagne will continue to campaign and to conquer (ll.522-28, 537-43, 550-556; note that the age of 200 years is not to be taken literally: it is part of Charlemagne's patriarchal image, cf. Methuselah and the Old Testament patriarchs). Ganelon replies that Charles is not himself warlike, and continues with praise of his lord (ll.529-36); in the second and third laisses (and this somewhat departs from the strictest *laisse similaire* pattern of e.g. ll.1051-81) the praise of the emperor is replaced by poisoned praise of Roland,

Oliver and the Peers. They are portrayed, once again, as the 'hawks' who keep the conflict alive; and the fact that they command the vanguard of 20,000 men, on whom Charles relies for his safety, is slipped in at the end of both laisses XLI and XLII. The poet, as so often, progressively increases precision on the most important element: to 'Carles n'est mie tels' (line 529) corresponds, first, 'Ço n'iert [...] tant cum vivet ses nies' (line 544) and then 'Ço n'iert [...] tant cum vivet Rollant' (line 557), the identity of the first words sharpening the impact when 'Roland' replaces 'his nephew'.

In XLIII, the important datum that the whole 400,000 strong Saracen army cannot withstand the Christian one is brought out again (cf. ll.17-19) by dramatic technique (ll.563-69): it is 'folie' to think of a trial of strength. Ganelon repeats the essentials of Blancandrin's plan (ll.570-73), but, for the conclusion that the French army will disband (cf. ll.49-50), he now substitutes another: the rearguard, in which Roland and Oliver will figure, he 'thinks' (line 575; how splendidly sinister that verb is! Ganelon is confident that he can manoeuvre them from van- to rearguard). The next lines are more explicit: if his advice is followed, the counts are dead men (*mort* is shockingly unambiguous at the head of line 577) and Charlemagne's fighting spirit will collapse. The plan is spelt out in XLIV, again in question-and-answer form. Starting with the rearguard, as in XLIII, Ganelon advises attacking the 20,000 with one quarter (100,000 men) of the Saracen host, once the emperor is up in the Ports de Cize. When the 100,000 have caused sufficient casualties, not without incurring heavy losses (ll.590-91), the remaining 300,000 should be able to mop up the rearguard and eliminate, with Roland, who must die in one or other of the attacks, Charles's ability to make war (ll.593-95). Laisse XLV emphasises this with a rare metaphor: Charles will have lost his 'right arm' (cf. ll.727, 1195; 1903, and cf. pp.42, 67 below) and the great army will disintegrate, never to be assembled again in a France (*Tere Major*) now intent on peace (ll.598-600). Marsile is delighted, kisses him and opens up his treasure.

Thus Ganelon brings together two plans of action: the withdrawal of the Franks (the limit of Blancandrin's idea) is now linked to the killing of Roland and the rearguard. Ganelon has succeeded in persuading the pagans that the first can be achieved only via the second. Four things can be brought out here. First, as has been said, the poet has used Ganelon *structurally* to bring Roland into the Saracen plot. Secondly, Ganelon has manoeuvred the pagans into this position and thinks he can use them as his weapon of revenge without involving treason towards Charles, or even Roland (cf. ll.3759-60, 3775-78). Thirdly, his plan depends on a correct assessment of Roland's character, which he will use to ensure that his stepson is in the rearguard, but on an incorrect judgement of Charlemagne, who precisely will not be debilitated by the loss of his 'right arm', but will, though heartbroken, take condign vengeance on Marsile's men and on Ganelon, not to mention Baligant (see van Emden, *159*, pp.179-81). Fourthly, the plan worked out here is strictly followed, down to the numbers involved (ll.715, 851, 1041, 1440); thus there is no need, as some have averred on the basis of other versions of the poem, for Marsile to be alerted to arrive as he does with the main army at line 1448.

In spite of his later denials (and point 2 above), Ganelon specifically swears treason against Roland on the relics of his sword (ll.605-08), so becoming guilty of a capital crime (line 608). The practice of sealing religious relics in the pommels of swords is exploited in greater detail at Roland's death (ll.2344-48); it appears to be a literary convention rather than a reflection of reality (*3*, n.2344-45; cf. however Edge and Paddock, *61*, p.46; Keen, *93*, p.53). It is noticeable that, unlike Isembart in *Gormont et Isembart*, Ganelon does not change his faith or his allegiance (cf. line 649). Thus an element of deception is involved (see especially laisse LIV; deceit and stealth are generally seen as constituent elements of treachery, cf. Mickel, *110*, pp.44, 73-87; van Emden, *164*, pp.318-28). This makes his action a crime at once less comprehensive than Isembart's and more difficult to forgive (van Emden, *154*, p.27). Marsile swears in his turn, on a book which (line 611) propagandistically traduces the Koran, that he will seek to kill Roland in the rearguard. This completes the planning of the treachery.

Laisses XLVIII-LII

The next three laisses, of which the first two are *parallèles* (see Chapter 4, p.107), show Ganelon receiving the kiss of Valdabrun and of Climborin, as well as rich gifts, in explicit (ll.623-24, 630-31) consideration of his treachery. Cook (*50*, pp.38-39) rightly emphasises the ignobleness of this; but there is no hint of avarice, any expectation of reward, before this point, *pace* Brault (*7*, pp.133, 135, etc.). The necklaces sent by Queen Bramimunde to Ganelon's wife (who, of course, is Charlemagne's sister, cf. line 640) constitute an unexpectedly naturalistic touch; Bramimunde, later called Bramidoine, will be the only pagan to be converted 'par amur' (ll.3674, 3975-87). If she can be converted after taking part in the treachery, is it incredible in principle that Marsile's apparently sincere request for Baptism should be considered or followed up? These three laisses in effect develop ll.601-02, and the kisses (very indirectly) and the treasures have Judas overtones. They above all serve to show that Ganelon cannot separate his vengeance from his duty towards Charles: he has sworn to help the Saracens to deceive the emperor and frustrate his projects.

The tribute and the high-born hostages are emphasised by the very short laisse LI, again through dramatic technique; laisse LII sums it all up: the complicity of Ganelon with the Saracens and the material rewards for it; the tribute, the keys of the city and the feigned submission to Charles (ll.654-55); the promise by Ganelon to get Roland into the rearguard and that of Marsile to kill him there. This leads into Ganelon's return.

Laisses LIII-LIV

The poet returns the audience to Charlemagne, awaiting Ganelon's return with the tribute (ll.665-66). Roland's military power and ruthlessness are summed up in the fate of an unidentified Spanish town, Galne, which he has laid waste for the next hundred years (cf. the story of Noples, ll.1775-79). The arrival of Ganelon at dawn is given an extra weight of suspense by filling the final line, which is then taken up again at the start of LIV, where Ganelon's words are delayed by Charlemagne's hearing of Mass and Mattins and the assembly of the council. Called traitor and perjuror by the indignant poet or narrator himself (line 674), Ganelon speaks with great cunning (*veisdie*). He first stresses the tribute, the keys and the hostages, but then lies brazenly to explain the absence of the caliph (ll.680-91), returning finally to the by now familiar promise of conversion and vassaldom. Charles thanks God as his first thought, and praises Ganelon, promising to reward him for his success; the French break camp and move off towards *dulce France*. It will be the caliph, under his name of Marganices, who will be there with his men to finish off the rearguard at ll.1913 ff., after the flight of Marsile and most of the pagan army; so Ganelon is further responsible for these deaths by his lies.

Laisse LV

This is a strange laisse: it sums up the campaign, now seen as closed, and recounts Charlemagne's departure, followed at once by what appears to be the first night's halt, signalled by Roland's raising the standard he has fixed (*fermee*), presumably to a lance shaft, on a hillock. But the army is being shadowed by 400,000 Saracens who wait for dawn hidden fully armed in a hilltop coppice, and the poet expresses his sorrow that the French are unaware of them (line 716). This is marvellously sinister, but puzzling: Marsile raises his 400,000 men at ll.848-55, taking three days over it. Further, Charles appears to set out for France at line 829. David Ross suggests (*136*, pp.173-77) that laisse LV is a relic of a previous version, closer to historical reality, which a reviser-poet has retained through inattention (or, one might suggest, because he liked the suspense it creates). If so, one must notice that the immediately following laisses LVI and LVII depend on night having fallen, as in LV, for they concern the first pair of prophetic dreams of Charlemagne.

Laisses LVI-LVII

The dreams of Charlemagne have been very variously interpreted by scholars (e.g. Steinmeyer, *146*; Braet, *38, 39, 40*; Owen, *119*; Whitehead, *171*; Hemming, *1*, n.719). They have to be seen, in the first place, as balanced by the later pair of dreams in laisses CLXXXV-CLXXXVI, which come before the battle against Baligant, just as the pair under discussion here precede the battle against Marsile. (Owen suggests that CLXXXVI was once part of the earlier sequence, but he has not persuaded most critics.) I continue to follow here my own interpretation (*158*): the precise details cannot be consistently interpreted across all the dreams, for the excellent reason that the author is too gifted to want to spell things out. He has created vaguely menacing visions (here again he is conforming, perhaps instinctively, to a classical pattern for presaging the fall of the great in tragedy); these increase the feeling of inevitability for the audience, as well as motivating Charlemagne's later fears after Roland's nomination. The laisse-boundary is deepened by the telling last line of LVI, LVII and CLXXXV: Charles cannot awake from each frightening dream.

The general pattern in each pair of dreams seems to be an evocation of the coming battle in the first laisse, followed by a second laisse in each case, foretelling the punishment of the traitor. Thus LVI, which takes place in dream time while Charles is in the Ports de Cize, represents the battle in Roncevaux, with Ganelon destroying the emperor's lance, a symbol which develops that of his right arm, and so designates Roland (ll.597, 727, 1195; cf. 835-40). LVII is not as easy to analyse, but it takes place in dream time, like that at CLXXXVI, when Charlemagne is back at Aix; the boar which attacks his right arm, Ganelon, is supported by a leopard, which must represent his defender Pinabel; when the hound comes leaping towards the sleeper, we do not at first know whether it is hostile too, but it then attacks the other two animals. The poet cleverly leaves the outcome in suspense (ll.734-35), as he does in the parallel dream at CLXXXVI, but the general pattern foretells the judicial combat about Ganelon's guilt. The vague menace and the uncertainty created by these dreams, which our poet is almost unique among his like in refusing to interpret for us, is masterly.

Laisses LVIII-LXIII

The coming of dawn, with the implicit awakening from the dreams, is deferred to the start of the next laisse: roused by bugles, the army sets off at once. The second nomination scene is, unexpectedly perhaps, played out on horseback (line 739). Referring to the intimidating landscape (line 741, cf. ll.814-15), Charles asks for nominations for the rearguard. Instantly, Ganelon seizes his chance to nominate Roland, his *cist miens fillastre* recalling the latter's evocation of the step-relationship at line 277, while his feigned praise similarly picks up that of the French for him at ll.278-79. This is another example of echo technique (cf. Heinemann, *80*, Troisième Partie; Suard, *148*, pp.4-5, 29-39), here serving to bring to mind the earlier nomination crisis as well as the fateful family link which underlies the hostility between the two. The king's reaction, conditioned by the dreams, is violent (ll.745-47; *vifs deables* may have Judas overtones again, cf. John 6. 70), but he is powerless to veto Roland (cf. ll.259-62) this time, since to do so would humiliatingly remove his nephew from a task exactly suited to his proven valour and experience, and that on no definite, avowable grounds. He assumes general agreement and turns to nominations for the vanguard, to which Ganelon appoints Ogier (the subject of an epic legend of his own) with praise echoing line 744 in a way apparently calculated to make his naming of Roland seem less noteworthy.

Roland's reaction spans two laisses of such contrasting tonality, at first sight, that it has been suggested that there is here evidence of contradiction, perhaps between two versions (see against this, with references, Bédier, *31*, III, pp.407, 426; Vinaver, *168*, pp.70-72). In fact, as Bédier says, Roland expresses ironic thanks to Ganelon in LIX, then his scorn (merely masked in LIX by the irony) in LX, though there is also an element of anger against his stepfather (cf. line 777). Both laisses express Roland's delight at being nominated; he confidently contrasts that delight with his stepfather's anger at his nomination for the embassy. One may relate them to what might be called 'the *similaire* technique': we have already looked at one series of *laisses similaires* (XL-XLII), and we shall examine others; here, rather than seeing the text as quoting two successive speeches, we may consider the same sentiments as being looked at from two contrasting (cf. ll.752, 762) points of view.

Roland states (laisse LIX) that Charles will suffer no losses – expressed in terms of kinds of riding animal – which will not have been paid for by the enemy with swords. Ganelon replies, with wonderfully suave irony, that Roland speaks the truth. Critics, myself included, have seen Roland's words as a characteristic expression of supreme confidence (cf. e.g. ll.1166-68), not to be taken literally. Robert Cook (*50*, pp.45-50) considers that, on the contrary, these words and those at ll.790-91 constitute Roland's understanding of his role as leader of a rearguard and his feudal promise to carry out what he says. He will stay and fight to the death if attacked, nothing more and nothing less: there is no promise of victory, only the statement that Charles need fear no man while his nephew is alive (line 791; this is seen as a 'careful qualification', p.50). Roland is not therefore free to choose at the moment of the first horn scene: he has already chosen and promised, and cannot sound the olifant without derogating from his duty as a vassal.

The problem for me with this very coherent theory is that it entails scrutinising Roland's words like some legal contract, to determine exactly what has, and has not, been promised. Nor does Roland refer to his alleged promises or to such limited objectives when he refuses to sound the horn: there he is quite confident of victory (ll.1055-58, 1065-69, 1077-81, cf. 1166-68), while Oliver consistently sees the decision not to recall the emperor as the crucial one (see ll.1099-1105, 1170-74, 1716-18, 1728-30); there is again no reference to Roland's words spoken at the moment of nomination.

The end of the rebuke in LX, the reminder of Ganelon's dropping the staff of office (in fact, it was the glove, ll.331-33: an example of the lack of consistency on details which oral performance allows) is developed in LXI as Roland asks for his own insignia of command, a bow. The emperor hesitates, showing his distress, and Naimon (LXII) has to urge him to action, advising Charles to find his nephew effective supporting forces (line 781). In LXIII, Roland is accordingly offered half the army, which he refuses. The offer is excessive, certainly, but the way it is rejected is significant: characteristically brusque (line 787), it is based on the fear of disgracing his family (line 788), a main motivation later (ll.1049-81) for his refusal to recall the emperor. The natural interpretation of ll.790-91 is that Charles can return in perfect safety since Roland is confident of complete success with the rearguard. I cannot see *a mun vivant* as a legalistic restriction, *pace* Cook, since Roland's death would on his own logic at once expose Charles to the danger which line 790 excludes.

Laisses LXIV-LXV

The 20,000 men, all that Roland will accept (line 789), as when he leads the vanguard, are chosen after eight of the twelve Peers, Turpin and Gualter del Hum have joined Roland and Oliver (for a complete list see ll.2402-09, where Astors is replaced by Samson). Gualter is a vassal of Roland's who is sent (LXV) to occupy the slopes of the defiles above the rearguard to prevent surprise attack (see Ross, *136*, on the tactical authenticity of this detail). He will return at the very end, after the death of all his men, his role being essentially to valorise that of Roland by his words at that point (ll.2045-46).

Laisses LXVI-LXVIII

As the army moves off into the passes, a recurrent description of the threatening setting appears for the first time (ll.814-15); echoes of it will recur at particularly critical moments (ll.1755, 1830-31, 2271). The distress of the army in its passage (ll.816-17) ends with the joy shown as the men see Gascony; their emotion at the thought of their homes and their womenfolk (ll.820-22) might conceivably be interpreted as battle-weariness, such as has been alleged by Brault and others, but it is natural enough not to need such explanation, and the high morale of the same men at the time of the decision is made clear in laisse VIII (see above pp.24-25).

Their tears lead into those of Charles, differently motivated and bringing some pathos to the narrative; the next laisse contrasts his anxiety with the confidence of the rearguard (ll.826-28) before Naimon's questions elucidate it in dramatic form. The fear induced by the dreams is used as a measure of Roland's unique value (line

840) and then extended to all the French in their worries for the rearguard in LXVIII (ll.841-43). The poet's comment about Ganelon's treason and the presents he has received from the Saracens leads smoothly to the latters' preparations. The raising of 400,000 men clashes, as we have seen above (p.41) with laisse LV, but underlines the vast superiority of the forces which now arrive within sight of the banners of the rearguard, whose readiness to fight is emphasised by the last lines of the laisse.

Laisses LXIX-LXXVIII

Twelve Saracen 'Peers', parallel to the French group, now emerge to promise Marsile the annihilation of the rearguard and Roland's death. After Marsile's nephew has been granted the first blow, there follow brief accounts of the twelve and their boasts. There is no space to analyse them here, but some general points can be made. The portraits are beautifully differentiated (contrast especially Margariz and Chernuble, ll.955-89), while the similarities in the boasts produce fine echo effects: the phrase *en Rencesvals* recurs like a refrain, emphasising the inhospitable nature of the battlefield, the 'valley of thorns' (ll.892, 901, 912, 923, 934, 944, 963, 985), and there are less insistent echoes on blood-stained weapons; most of the boasts also include the intended death of Roland, and, slightly less often, Oliver and the Peers (cf. Rychner, *138*, pp.90-91). Finally, the Saracen 'Peers' fight and die (ll.1188-1337 – with the exception of Margariz, who disappears in the press, ll.1318-19) in the same order in which they make their boasts here: the narrative is clearly planned with care.

Laisse LXXIX

The parade of individual Saracen 'Peers' widens out into a description of the arming of the pagans (see *1*, n.994-98); the colours of the banners (line 999) and the gleaming of the armour (line 1003) are an example of the poet's pleasure in colour, texture and reflections (Bennett, *34*), and the idealisation climaxes in the thousand bugles which blow 'por ço que plus bel seit'. This last detail is simple ornamentation: even pagan bugles add to the idealised beauty of the text! But the poet also uses them to transfer the hearer's attention from the Saracens to the Christians. The next line (1005) is the exact centre of the laisse, which pivots on it: in the first hemistich, we are with the Saracens; in the second, we are transferred, with the sound, to the French, among whom Oliver is the first to realise its meaning. Roland is delighted at the prospect of fighting and gives his feudal warrior's credo, his ideal of sacrificial vassalic service (ll.1009-14), which he will echo (ll.1117-19) after the 'horn scene' that is about to start.

Janet Boatner (*35*) rightly stresses that the feudal does not exclude the Christian, quite the contrary; but those who see Roland as a *christomimetes*, moved by the Folly of the Cross, need to account for the fact that the hero expresses himself in terms so consistently feudal that other scholars can argue for an almost pre-Christian conception of this hero, in short, that he mentions God so little. This is especially striking if he is compared with Vivien in the first part (which preserves a poem almost as old as *Roland*, and influenced by it) of the *Chanson de Guillaume* (particularly *21*, ll.204-07, 249-51, see van Emden, *157*, pp.27-30). Vivien, who is represented as motivated mainly by his Christian faith, is placed in a similarly hopeless military position, but carefully kept clear of any responsibility by the way the *Guillaume* is structured.

This contrast does not imply that Roland is represented as unchristian or lacking faith, only that the *Roland* poet has made his dominant motivation more feudal than strictly religious. It is significant that Archbishop Turpin will shortly express a similarly feudal sentiment (ll.1127-28), but will add the Christian dimension unspoken by Roland (ll.1129-35). The famous line 1015 'Paien unt tort e chrestïens unt dreit' is often quoted to show Roland's Christian zeal but, *pace* Hemming (*1*, n.1015), it may just as well refer to the Saracens' breach of their word. A very similar line, 1212, occurs in the specific rebuttal of Aelroth's taunts of feudal betrayal by Charlemagne in leaving the rearguard behind. (Brault's alternative view (*7*, p.192), that the treason referred to is Ganelon's, is at least as helpful to my argument. It is true that line 3554 is possibly to be read on the religious level: see Chapter 3, p.88). In any case, Roland's dominant tone, concern with military reputation, is reflected before and after, in ll.1014, 1016, as is rightly stressed by Short's comment on line 1014: 'Roland a la hantise de la honte, et ne peut supporter l'idée d'être sanctionné par la mémoire collective aristocratique. L'obsession revient aux vv.1466 et 1472' (cf. also Short's n.1053).

The next two laisses show Oliver climbing a hill to confirm his suspicions. The poet describes the pagan host through his eyes, in terms first of the reflections of light from the armour (ll.1021-22, made more insistent by the echoes and anaphoric repetitions in ll.1031-33), then of sheer numbers: he cannot count even the divisions (*escheles*, line 1034). Between the *similaire* passages devoted to this comes his accusation against Ganelon; at this stage, before battle is joined, Roland's family honour forbids any acceptance of the accusation (cf., however, ll.1145-49). Oliver returns, *mult esguarét*, 'disturbed', 'shattered', according to one's translator, even 'distraught' (if one is to adopt Moignet's Modern French use of *égaré*). Cook (*50*, p.63) makes much of this to disparage Oliver, but the context shows it to be no more than a natural reaction at seeing 100,000 armed men – and these are just the ones in view (line 1041) – approaching. For after a further description of the Saracens, Oliver soberly accepts that an unprecedented fight awaits them, and calmly exhorts the French, who respond positively, to stand their ground to prevent defeat (ll.1044-46, cf. ll.1175-79; for support for this interpretation, see Brault, *7*, p.177).

Laisses LXXXIII-LXXXV

These stanzas, the 'First Horn Scene', constitute another series of *laisses similaires*, the most celebrated example in the Old French epic. Apart from the lyrical intensity such patterns of repetition inject into the narrative (cf. Rychner, *138*, Chap. IV; Suard, *148*, pp.29-39; we will return to poetic technique in Chapter 4), they are also, if they involve dialogue, part of the dramatic method of exposition. The repeated statement of points of view in opposition to each other draws the issues involved to the attention of the hearers, and may challenge them to judge between the speakers.

Laisses LXXXIII-LXXXV are, as distinct from XL-XLII, completely static. This is because (perhaps in a threefold look at *one* conversation) they show an argument which is not a meeting of minds: the two friends speak on parallel planes and represent two mutually exclusive points of view. Thrice Oliver's call for Roland to sound the olifant to bring back the army is refused in identical, though increasingly passionate, terms. (In this energetic rejection, the evocation of God's Name at ll.1062, 1073 is little more than another way of saying 'Jo fereie que fols'; one can hardly hang an argument for Roland's Christian enthusiasm on such standard expressions; 'ne placet Damnedeu' is later put in Pinabel's mouth, line 3906, cf. line 3768.) There follows an argument based on reputation (ll.1054, 1063-64, 1074-76), widening out from Roland's own to that of his relations and France itself; then an evocation of great blows to be struck with his sword Durendal (ll.1055-56, 1065-67, 1077-79), whose name recurs each time, together with the motif of blood on its blade; finally, in the last two lines of each stanza, a confident prediction of the total defeat and death of the pagans. (The last lines of the next five laisses all repeat the theme of striking great blows, making eight in all.) The expression becomes increasingly personal: the use of first person singular verbs, some with the personal pronoun (optional in Old French), and the possessive adjectives *mun*, *mi*, all increase the personal accent, from the very first word, *Jo*, to the almost solipsistic series in ll.1077-79, where Roland seems practically to forget that anyone else will be fighting at all (cf. Jonin, *89*).

The confidence (cf. ll.1166-68) is misplaced: however brave the French (line 1080), they will not be able to win given the odds against them, and we shall see them all killed except Roland. How are we to interpret the hero's confidence, which the poem itself shows to be untenable? In assessing Roland's responsibility for the disaster, we must remember that the poet makes it clear (ll.18-19, 564-69) that the entire Saracen army cannot withstand Charlemagne's at full strength. Cook (*50*, p.64) argues that Roland does not claim that the Saracens will be killed there, by his own hand and the efforts of his men, only that they are doomed to die;

but if one reads these lines in the context of what precedes (especially ll.1080-81), this is to go against the clear grain of the text. Roland is shown as sure of victory. But, even on Cook's assumption, if Charles is thus expected to finish the killing in any case, why does Roland not call him back at once, thus minimising casualties and ensuring victory? There seems to be no textual evidence for Foulet's theory that a battle-weary Charles has to be forced, by Roland's sacrifice of himself and the twenty thousand, to finish the campaign; and, if Cook were right in seeing Roland, as a mediaeval man, bound by his promises made at the nomination, with their 'careful qualifications' (Cook, *50*, p.50), why does that other mediaeval man, Oliver, not understand?

Everything about the scene just analysed seems calculated to show Roland making his decision for reasons of personal and familial honour, seeing it as shaming to call for help even though faced with enormous odds. (It is misleading to argue, as has been done, that these are only five to one: Oliver says (line 1041) that those he can see at the front number 100,000: it is obvious that there are many more behind.) And one can only interpret Roland's baseless certainty about victory as arising from a hubristic excess of confidence (Oliver will call it 'recklessness', ll.1725-26), a *desmesure* natural enough after his past victories, but which is the fault causing his error or *hamartia*: the refusal to send for aid while there is still time. To say this is not to undermine Roland's status as hero; on the contrary, it is to explain how he comes to be a tragic one.

Laisses LXXXVI-LXXXVIII

The argument continues along the same lines in the next laisses: Oliver cannot understand Roland's scruple in the face of the odds (ll.1082-87). On the point of honour involved here, see van Emden, *157*: it is clear from analysis of the start of the *Chanson de Guillaume* that there is no shame in deferring a battle, or sending for aid, if the odds are overwhelming, provided this is done before the fighting has started. Oliver is consistent on this: he sees no problem at this point, and he sees every problem when Roland, at the height of the battle, wishes to call Charles back (laisses

CXXVIII-CXXXI, see below, pp.61-64). For Roland, the odds are an extra incentive (line 1088) and he just repeats the point about shame (which Oliver cannot accept as being relevant) with the feudal comment that it is for great blows that Charlemagne loves them.

Still there is no meeting of minds: there are two different conceptions of honour involved, and this impasse is perhaps what the author wants to underline in the famous lines at the start of LXXXVII: 'Rollant est proz e Oliver est sage,/Ambedui unt meveillus vasselage' (ll.1093-94). Much ink has been spilt over these lines (e.g. Bédier, *31*, III, pp.432-34; Burgess, *44*, pp.91-103; Brault, *7*, pp.180-83, *41*; Guiette, *75*, pp.850-55; Misrahi/Henderson, *112*, pp.366-67; cf. *113*, pp.229-30; Cook, *50*, p.70; Venckeleer, *167*, pp.363, 463-65). There is no space to take up the divergent readings here. Many interpretations have treated the conjunction *e* as though it were *mais*, as Brault (*41*, p.90) points out. But a commonsense approach to the line in the context of what has just been narrated and what is to follow suggests that two contrasting qualities are implied, not necessarily in opposition, but perhaps seen to complement each other, at least if we agree with Bédier that Oliver was created at some point in the development of the legend to act as a foil to Roland. I continue to see *proz* as describing the quality which makes the latter the hero of the poem: courage combined with total commitment to what he believes to be right; *sage* describes, in spite of the Misrahi/Henderson argument of 'guilt by association' (see pp.28, 33 above), the prudent wisdom displayed by Oliver here and elsewhere.

It is idle to speculate as to which the poet 'prefers', indeed the question is meaningless unless we ask on what plane the preference lies. It is obvious that, on a purely tactical level, Oliver is right (van Emden, *159*, pp.175-77), since a returning Charlemagne and the army would inevitably defeat the Saracens (ll.17-18, 564-69). But on a literary level, Roland's refusal to count the cost, his charisma, his larger-than-life ability to go to the limit of commitment and his military prowess make him the hero of the poem, to be 'preferred' in that sense to Oliver (cf. Guiette, *75*, p.852: 'ce qui lui manque [à

Olivier], c'est la folie'; cf. also Kay, *90*). The poet in any case hastens to complete his intervention with the point that *both* have courage to marvel at, both will continue to fight to the death once they have begun. But it is incontrovertible that Oliver does not see the point of dying for personal, family and national glory (cf. ll.1731-36), especially when he does not share Roland's assessment of where honour lies: he will later ask Roland just what sort of vassalic service it is to deprive the king of 20,000 of his best men, and above all of himself.

'Bon sunt li cunte e lur paroles haltes' perhaps sums up the situation as well as ll.1093; both are admirable and their conflict befits an epic. Some time is now assumed to have passed, for when Oliver speaks again, it is too late to recall Charles (line 1100). For the first of three times, Oliver uses the verb *deignier* of Roland's refusal to sound the horn: 'Vostre olifan suner vos ne.l deignastes' (line 1101, cf. ll.1171, 1716), so it is clear that he believes his friend's conduct to be motivated by pride; the reproach is associated each time with the incontrovertible statement that, had the king been with them, the victory would have been theirs without the loss of the rearguard. Roland comes near to calling him a coward (ll.1106-07), but in the next laisse his tone to Oliver softens (ll.1113, 1120) as he grows in fierceness towards the enemy and repeats his ideal of costly feudal service (ll.1117-19). The rift between the comrades is now considerable, but the boil will not be lanced until the Second Horn Scene (ll.1691-1752), when Oliver will make Roland understand his anger in precise terms; in the meantime, one has the impression that the poet has Roland try repeatedly to make his friend talk reassuringly to him, but with minimal success (ll.1146-51, 1360-77, 1395, 1456-66, 1545-48, 1558-61, 1671-76). Cook (*50*, pp.71-72) draws attention to Roland's concession (line 1122) that he may die, and remarks that it fits badly with the *desmesure* hypothesis. It is difficult to see why: Roland is confident of the rearguard's winning, but to exclude the possibility of not living to see it would be absurd, and presuppose an invulnerability which would remove any need for courage (cf. van Emden, *157*, pp.38-39). The subordinate clause in any case leads on to a main clause which characteristically stresses Roland's preoccupation with his own reputation.

Laisses LXXXIX-XC

The preparation for the battle continues with Archbishop Turpin's speech. We have already seen that he speaks at first feudally like Roland (ll.1127-28), but then adds a Christian dimension largely lacking in Roland's language. He absolves the French from their sins and promises them the status of martyrs if they fall. In this, he echoes the preaching of the First Crusade by Pope Urban II at Clermont in 1095, as it was (mis)understood by contemporaries (Mayer, *109*, pp.30-37; cf., apart from the conclusions about the supposed incestuous origin of Roland, Mölk, *115*). In the next stanza, Roland is at last ready to accept what Oliver had said earlier about Ganelon's treachery: it would seem that, once the decision has been taken, there is no further obstacle of family solidarity (for a different interpretation, see Brault, *7*, pp.177-78; Brault is right to point out that their conclusion has to be intuitive, since it is not based on any firm evidence). The realisation is turned into a grim and effective call to arms in yet another fine end of laisse (ll.1150-51, cf. line 1138).

Laisses XCI-XCII

As Roland, riding his horse which is traditionally called Viellantif, reaches the passes of Spain, we see him in his glory, carrying out an *eslais*, or morale-raising gallop (cf. ll.3165-71, 3341-44) before his men. The splendid picture was imitated in later poems, such as the *Guillaume*, and the sight of him causes his men to acclaim him as their *guarant* (line 1161). This word is a key concept (see van Emden, *157*, pp.37-45): briefly, the commander of a force takes the place of the members' feudal lord and becomes their *guarant* (even if they are not his vassals normally) and has the lord's duties: he must bolster his men's morale, he is expected to choose the time of the battle for the best prospects of victory, to protect and aid his warriors and, if they nevertheless die, to mourn (speak a *planctus* over them) and avenge them. The key requirement in our context is obviously the choice of when to fight, which, as ll.168-82 of the *Guillaume* show, involves the calculation of relative numerical strength and the advisability of sending for reinforcements. This is precisely the ground of the dispute between Roland and Oliver, and we shall see later (ll.1863-64) how important Roland's role of *guarant* is to the poet and to our judgement of his responsibility.

For the moment, Roland is doing exactly what the *guarant* should do: he raises morale by looking fiercely at the Saracens and, with gentleness and the humility of the commander who recognises the value of his men, at the French (ll.1162-63), threatening the enemy and promising his warriors immense booty from the defeat of the pagans (ll.1166-68). We know from ll.396-99 that it is Roland's habit to share the booty with his men – a major reason for his popularity with them – but it has to be pointed out that here he is making a promise which he cannot keep (unless we interpret *eschec* in improbable ways, as do Brault, *7*, pp.187-88, Cook, *50*, pp.74-75). Roland's assessment of the situation is in this respect demonstrably skewed by a confidence which Oliver, for one, will later ascribe to folly, recklessness and lack of *mesure* (ll.1724-26). The argument about the nature of Roland's role is essentially one about the accuracy of the views put in the mouth of Oliver by the poet.

The *eslais* commonly leads straight into the start of fighting, and there is no exception here: the armies engage in the last lines of both XCI and XCII, so time as it were stands still while Oliver repeats his reproaches. He makes the important point that Charles and the main army (*Cil ki la sunt*, line 1174) have no responsibility for what will happen (cf. line 1718; see Burger, *42*, pp.111-13). It is entirely Roland's. But having said his piece, Oliver loyally turns to the French with encouragement, to which they respond enthusiastically and then gallop into battle.

Laisse XCIII

The first combat involves couched lances, a phase which logically precedes use of the sword, once the former are shattered. The next 450 or so lines are largely taken up with single combats, interspersed with general views of the battle and other forms of variation. It is clear that the description of great blows, involving epic exaggeration, was popular with the hearers, and the series of encounters does indeed add up to an impressive evocation of a bloody battle, but there is no need to analyse each such laisse in detail; only one sample, and other significant information, will be commented on. Heavy cavalry has no imaginable defensive role and, as Cook (*50*, pp.75-76) pertinently comments, 'no battlefield function to speak of, except vigorous attack'. This may well be the sense of line 1185. The opening combat, involving Roland and Aelroth, nephew of Marsile, who had been granted the first blow (ll.866-873), is more detailed than others and may illustrate the use of the lance.

The attack by Aelroth, riding ahead of the army, is preceded by a scornful boast: the French have been betrayed by their *guarant*, the one (Charlemagne) who had them in his protection, and who is mad for leaving them in the passes. Today France will lose her fame, and Charles his right arm (we have seen that this symbolises Roland, cf. ll.597, 727). This enrages Roland (line 1196) who spurs his horse to the gallop and strikes the Saracen with all his force. The couched lance breaks Aelroth's shield and tears open his hauberk (mail coat), pierces his chest and shatters his bones, cutting through the spine; the spear sunders his soul from his body. Roland strikes Aelroth's body down, sending it toppling dead with levelled lance (?: on *pleine sa hanste* see *1*, n.1204, but there have been many interpretations of this common phrase). The neck is broken in half (somewhat superfluously!). The killing is followed by a refutation of every point of Aelroth's boast, spoken over the dead body, and a final two lines of encouragement to the Franks, now that the first blow has been victoriously struck. The blow and its effects are standard parts of the motif, at least in its fuller forms (cf. Rychner, *138*, pp.139-49), the order of which is of course dictated to a large degree by reality (however exaggerated). The taunt over the body of the enemy is also common: in an age characterised by what I have elsewhere called 'ordeal-mindedness' (van Emden, *160*, p.173; cf. Morris, *116*, p.104; Scully, *142*), the result of such single combats, especially where the enemy has made challenges like

Aelroth's, is seen as a vindication of the Christian champion, parallel to the outcome of a *judicium Dei*, a formal judicial combat.

Laisses XCIV-CIV

In turn, other Franks fight similar victorious combats against the Saracen 'Peers', following the order in which the latter speak in the scene before Marsile (ll.860-993). The second and third duels, Oliver's and Turpin's, receive equally detailed, parallel treatment with Roland's, together with which they form a set of *laisses parallèles* replicating the judicial combat in form (Scully, *142*). Most of the Franks concerned in the duels are Peers, though Turpin is not, nor is Gualter (del Hum?) at ll.1297-1303. Roland and Oliver have two encounters each (the second at ll.1320ff. and ll.1311ff. respectively) in which the former kills a second pagan 'Peer', Chernuble, but Oliver, attacked but not wounded by Margariz, seems not to return his assailant's blow. Margariz disappears from the poem, sounding his bugle to rally his forces. Unlike Michael Hecht (*77*, pp.91-93, 109-10) I see in this anomalous combat no depreciation of Oliver, who already has one comprehensive victory to his credit, and is spared by God's special protection in what sounds like a surprise attack (line 1316). The reason is no doubt to be sought in Margariz's role, in versions other than Oxford, of fetching Marsile and the main part of the pagan army for the second phase of the battle as planned earlier (ll.583-95). It would seem probable, given Margariz's escape, that *O* has deliberately omitted this feature, and there is much to be said for such a decision, since the Saracen plan has been carefully laid and is carried out precisely. On this hypothesis, the non-*O* versions would here have the original disposition of the narrative, but *O* would contain an innovation which is also an improvement.

Laisses CV-CIX

Here we have the first slightly more general view of the battle, in that these laisses do not recount single combats in detail but pass quickly over a number of victories by the Peers and Turpin, with admiring comments from others. The fact that Oliver is still using, to great effect, the stump of his shattered lance (line 1352) allows

Roland to address him humorously and suggest he draw his sword Hauteclere. With a brief reply which memorably encapsulates the heat of the battle, Oliver does so and, in laisse CVII, provides a typical combat with the sword, which may stand for others. The victim is named in the first line; then follows the blow, epic, not realistic: it cuts the pagan's head vertically, then divides the body with its mail coat and the saddle to split the horse's spine and so hurl both (so I interpret *tut*) dead on to the meadow before him (ll.1370-75). Roland admires the blow, receiving no further reply, but the French shout Charlemagne's battle-cry in enthusiastic response.

After a further laisse of varied, and rather exotic, successes (including a double attack by the Peers Gerin and Gerer and the death of a wizard who has visited hell through Jupiter's sorcery), we return in CIX to a general view of the fierce (*aduree*) battle. The evocation of damage to equipment involving anaphoric repetition of *tant* (ll.1399-1400) leads in line 1401 to the same word emphasising the number of young French warriors who are dying. This is the first mention of Christian casualties and the end of the laisse evokes the loss to their loved ones and their comrades waiting for them in the passes.

Laisses CX-CXIII

The reference to the passes leads naturally to a description of Charlemagne's continuing anxiety and a crushing statement that there can be no help for the rearguard, though there will be punishment (ll.1408-09 – inaccurately prophesied, cf. ll.3964-73) for Ganelon. The last two lines of CIX and the first of CX are beautifully echoed in the next laisse, at ll.1421-22, with their lyrical evocation of those who will wait in vain for the French dead (cf. pp.108-09). Yet these follow ll.1412-19, from which we learn that the Saracens are dying in far greater numbers and that those who do not flee are all being killed; the battle appears almost over. So ll.1421-22 move us from this high point to a passage of premonition on a cosmic scale, in which the whole of France (for toponyms and implications, see *1*, n.1428-29) is visited by terrifying storms and earthquakes (ll.1423-34). While Hemming (n.1431) is right to point to parallels from scriptural accounts of the phenomena accompanying Christ's death on the Cross (Matthew 27. 45, 51 and Luke 23. 44-45), the poet himself points us to the *Parousia*, the Second Coming of Christ (line 1435; cf. Joel 2. 10, Matthew 24. 29, Revelation 6. 12, etc.). So Roland's coming death reflects, in its cosmic consequences, those of both Crucifixion and *Parousia*; that is to say that the significance of his death is given truly epic recognition. Bédier (*32*, p.314) points also to the portents of Caesar's assassination in the *Aeneid*, which the poet may well have known: in general terms, the death of heroes in epic and tragedy is often foreshadowed by cosmic signs.

Laisse CXII repeats the temporary triumph of the French (for the *Geste Francor*, line 1443, cf. ll.1685, 3262, 3742 as a fictional but prestigious source, see *1*, n.1443). As the survivors seek out their own dead for burial (usually a sign that a battle is over), Marsile with his great host (the remaining 300,000 Saracens) suddenly appears (*lor surt*, literally 'rises up upon them', line 1448).

At this point, two dotted lines in the Whitehead edition (maintained by Hemming) indicate the conviction that a passage, present in other versions and relating the ride of Margariz to inform Marsile of the situation, had been omitted in *O*. The anomalous survival of Margariz in *O* makes this very possible, as has been said; nevertheless, there is no indication of any gap in the manuscript, and there is no narrative need for the message: Marsile (who is already on the scene before the hypothetical gap) is simply carrying out the plan arranged at ll.570-95, and if the person responsible for *O* decided to omit the message episode, we may think that the poem benefited thereby. (Detailed discussion in *6*, pp.185-88.)

Laisse CXIII continues logically from the end of CXII, the opening developing line 1448 by describing the splendour of Marsile's twenty divisions in characteristic terms of reflected light from armour and the great sound of many bugles; this leads equally naturally to Roland's reaction, who accepts again Ganelon's part in this and encourages a silent Oliver. The desire not to lose reputation is still uppermost (line 1466).

Laisses CXIV-CXVI

The Archbishop dominates these laisses, the opening of which again follows directly from the preceding material. Marsile takes in the extent of the slaughter of his first wave, and launches the attack, which is led by Abisme. After a description of this strikingly unattractive pagan, the Archbishop begins the second phase (line 1487) by fighting and killing him. When the French, after exulting for a moment in his victory, are discouraged by the number of the Saracens (ll.1510-11 picking up ll.1448, 1449-55), Turpin assures them of their heavenly reward (now certain, ll.1519-23, where it was still hypothetical at ll.1134-35); French morale rises at once (ll.1524-25).

In spite of the coherence of this account, many editors here follow the very different order of the non-*O* manuscripts (see the numbers in the right-hand margin of *1*). This is done mainly on stylistic grounds (see Segre, *5*, pp.310-11, *6*, pp.215-16) which do not convince me, if only because Turpin's 'starting the battle' (line 1487) is thereby pushed nearly 200 lines from the actual beginning of the second phase. Once again, with the possible exception of two successive laisses on one assonance, CXXV and CXXVa, which many editors (e.g. Bédier, Moignet) rearrange, *O* seems to me to have the best text of this episode; in this case, I believe it is in general the original order too, and Whitehead was right to maintain it.

There are several admirable features of laisses CXIV-CXVI worthy of notice, though space forbids analysis: the detailed description (ll.1470-80) of Abisme, standard-bearer to Marsile, worthy of comparison with those of Margariz and Chernuble; the delightful understatement with which Turpin decides to fight him (ll.1481-86); the description of the Archbishop's horse (ll.1488-96), which obeys strict rules of descriptive technique (see Chapter 4, p.122) and contains elements from Isidore of Seville's *Etymologies* (cf. Bédier, *32*, p.304, and Faral, *65*, pp.198-201) – both factors suggesting the culture of the poet; the amusing (only to us?) logic of ll.1508-09, which shows clearly the epic preference for the military over the clerical (cf. ll.1876-82!); Turpin's solemn, totally realistic

promise of death that day, and Paradise, which raises the morale of
the Franks (ll.1515-23; cf. ll.1127-35 and p.53 above).

Laisses CXVII-CXXV

Assuming the original order to be that of *O*, we see parallels
and contrasts with the first phase: the first encounter is again a
success for the French, and it is followed by a series of single
combats involving some of the Twelve Peers (CXVII-CXXV). Only
this time it is the Peers who are killed, six of them, mourned by the
Franks and avenged each time by Oliver, Roland or Turpin. In the
first combats of the previous phase, these heroes fought in the order
Roland, Oliver, Turpin (XCIII-XCV); here, starting with the
Abisme combat, the order is reversed (CXV-CXX); such patterns
are perhaps extra evidence for the authenticity of *O*'s text.

There is no point in analysing these laisses closely: they
correspond to the two types, lance and sword, examined earlier,
though it is interesting that the poet has not forgotten that the
Saracen attackers are fresh, so he makes them attack with the lance,
while vengeance comes each time with the sword (though ll.1610-
12 are ambiguous). The Saracens are presented with individualising
detail (ll.1529-33, 1562-70 – it seems Muslims too are baptised! –,
ll.1593-98, 1613-16), and the Christian avengers are further
distinguished by comment, mainly from participants (ll.1508-09,
1558-60, 1590, 1608-09; line 1652 refers to Roland's role as
guarant, and the hero is particularly valorised by the reaction of
Grandonie, 1636-43).

Laisses CXXVa-CXXVII

These three laisses (if we separate CXXVa from CXXV, see
1, n.1653-60) lead into the Second Horn Scene by reducing the
Christian army rapidly to a handful. In whichever order CXXVa
and CXXVI were originally written, the effect is to give the
impression that the Christians are still winning and the Saracens in
disarray. But when a new Frankish attack is launched by Roland
(ll.1671-77) we learn that the tide turns. In spite of their efforts, and
especially those of Roland, Oliver and Turpin (ll.1680-85 – with
another appeal to the mysterious *Gesta* (*Francorum*) which is

alleged as source, cf. ll.1443, 2095, 3262, 3742), the fifth onset proves disastrous after four successful ones. There are only sixty French warriors left.

Laisses CXXVIII-CXXXII

The Second Horn Scene is much less precisely structured than the first, partly because there is now some meeting of minds and some movement; this is a dynamic passage, containing much echo and parallelism (some of it with the First Horn Scene) but no real *laisses similaires*. At line 1691, Roland seems suddenly to waken to the disaster which has occurred (there was no sign of awareness in his previous speech, ll.1672-75). He calls out to Oliver and, after bewailing the loss, surprises us by regretting the absence of Charlemagne (line 1697), whom he has so deliberately decided not to recall, and asks how news might be sent to him. Oliver replies brusquely that he does not know and that he prefers to die rather than to incur shame.

For the detail of my interpretation of this discussion, I must refer to my articles (*157, 162*). That Oliver should refer at once to shame as something to avoid is not simply an angrily ironic allusion to Roland's own position in the First Horn Scene and after. It can be elucidated from the first part of the *Chanson de Guillaume*, where it is made very evident that, while a *guarant* may, indeed should, send for help before fighting has started if the military odds warrant it, it becomes shameful so to do once the battle has begun, even technically (see *21*, ll.49-58, 70-74, 113-22 compared with ll.192-211, 252-58).

This parallel account in *Guillaume* illuminates *Roland*'s laisse CXXIX, and sheds a (for us) retrospective light on the First Horn Scene, from which ll.1703-04 are textually repeated (cf.ll.1071-72, down to the details of spelling), only now they are spoken by Roland instead of Oliver. The latter had used them to urge the recall of Charles for help, and it is clear that Roland now uses them for the same purpose. Oliver immediately rejects the proposition, and his reference to the shame which would fall on them and on Roland's family is again more than an expression of bitterness. The parallel from the *Guillaume* shows that his conclusion at ll.1710-11 makes a very serious point, though we have to follow Hoepffner (*82*, p.243, n.3) in substituting a colon for the full stop placed after line 1710 in most editions (Segre, *6* and Short, *9*, 2nd edn, excepted). The fact that Roland has his arms covered with blood is the justification for the assertion that sounding the horn will not be the act of a brave man: the battle has well and truly started, and so sending for help would indeed be shameful. (The readings of the *Rhymed Roland* manuscripts *P*, *T* and – in spite of a contrary reading based on misunderstanding – *L* make the point very explicit: *P*: '"[...]Car li corners n'est or mie avenans,/ Puis que sainglens en est li vostres brans"', *11*, ll.1651-52.) For an explanation of the rationale of this convention, see Burger, *43*, p.138: 'En voyant Roland sonner du cor, les bras couverts de sang, les derniers survivants perdront courage; ils comprendront qu'il désespère de la victoire, "que Rollant se dementet" comme dira le duc Naimes à l'ouïe de la voix du cor, et la bataille risque de se terminer par un sauve-qui-peut; ce serait grande vergogne.' For a slightly divergent view, also linking ll.1710 and 1711, see Sutherland, *149*; cf. also *Guillaume*, *21*, ll.202-06.)

As in the first scene. the theme of blowing the horn is repeated at the start of the second laisse of the set of three, and meets with refusal (though of course with roles inverted). Oliver's objection redoubles the accusation of a dishonouring lack of courage (line 1715) and, now with echoes of his own words in the aftermath to the first scene (ll.1716-18, cf. ll.1101-02, 1171-74), repeats the implicit accusation of pride with the verb *deignier* and points out again that Charles could have ensured victory without disastrous losses. That Oliver should speak again immediately (line 1719), after another 'Dist Oliver', may imply a lacuna, though the other assonanced version, *V4*, has roughly the same text, but without the *verbum dicendi*. In any case. the second part of Oliver's speech precipitates the final explanation, which one might go so far as to call the moment of truth. Oliver, in his anger, says that if they get out of this alive, he will veto Roland's projected marriage to his sister Aude. This would be less as her brother than as Roland's comrade in arms, his *cumpainz* (cf. ll.324, 1723; for the archaic, by

1100 probably literary, institution of *compagnonnage*, which appears to have a Germanic origin, and, in its 'higher degree', entered into with formal vows, bound comrades to share all dangers, avenge each other and not to marry without the other's consent, see Stowell, *147*; G.F. Jones, *88*, pp.114, 143).

It is possible to understand this threat as a desire to distance himself from a man about to incur dishonour, or simply as a measure of Oliver's anger, which is how Roland, at the start of laisse CXXXI, the third in the series, takes it. To his almost naïve question 'Por quei me portez ire?' he receives the shatteringly simple answer 'Cumpainz, vos le feïstes', followed by a burningly lucid assessment of Roland's error. Courage not moderated by prudence leads to folly (line 1724); *mesure* (see above, p.19) is better than recklessness, which is the cause of the death of the French (ll.1725-26); Charlemagne will never again have feudal service from any of them (ll.1726, 1732 – Roland, after all, had been the one to exalt the duties of the vassal); had Charles returned, the battle would have been won and Marsile killed or taken (ll.1728-30), so that the display of Roland's prowess has been a disaster for them all (line 1731). Above all, Roland's own coming death will bring shame to France: Oliver's anger is clearly fuelled by his love for his friend and by his frustration at the waste of Roland's splendid life. Their deaths will before evening end their *compagnonnage* (ll.1735-36).

We may wonder whether we are thinking anachronistically if we agree with Oliver against Roland; if so, we should note that the author gives Roland no answer to this devastating assessment. Bédier (*31*, III, p.439) saw this as the moment of truth: '[Roland] se tait, et ce silence est la chose la plus sublime de *La Chanson de Roland*'. Many later critics have been dismissive of this view, but one must ask oneself whether, had the author seen Roland as being morally in the right, he would have let the argument end on this powerful endictment.

Not only does this seem to offer confirmation of Roland's tragic error, but the scene, by its very structure, suggests that the hero has come to a realisation of its consequences and a determination to do what he can to expiate it, whatever the cost. If he and Oliver have been arguing about recalling Charlemagne to save what is left of the rearguard, and if this action would be dishonouring, then Roland is now ready to accept for himself and his family the shame which he had been so trenchantly unwilling to incur in the First Horn Scene. Such a 'U-turn' argues at the least a radical change of perception, which one might well call repentance, and the desire to mitigate the damage for which he realises he is responsible.

Of course, the poet cannot allow his hero to be dishonoured, and the next laisse uses Turpin to put matters in their right perspective. Critics have been too ready to say that the Archbishop sides with Roland (e.g. Brault, 7, pp.212-13; Cook, 50, pp.88-89; Short, 9, n.1702). He rebukes both of the quarrelling friends. Certainly, he agrees that the horn should be sounded, but not to bring aid: it is too late for that, and the only possible purpose is to fetch vengeance and ensure Christian burial for them all (ll.1742-51). This is something neither Roland nor Oliver has mentioned, and it is arbitrary for Brault to say that Turpin 'merely echoes the hero's sentiments' in making his point. Roland could indeed have motivated his idea in this way from the beginning of the argument, but the poet has chosen instead to let both the friends pursue a 'non-argument' on the level of calling for help, delaying the obvious answer until he has made it clear that Roland is actually willing to accept the dishonour involved. And this can only be because the author wishes the audience to see that Roland now regrets his earlier decision and wishes to mitigate its consequences. Here, as with the silence of Ganelon, it is the very structure of the narrative that shows the poet's intention.

Laisses CXXXIII-CXXXV

Roland's sounding of the olifant is related in three further *laisses similaires*, with much echo (appropriately!) and incremental repetition (see Chapter 4, pp.107-12, 114-16), though they are not very tightly structured. The first, shortest laisse stresses the distance the call has to cover and the power Roland deploys; the second and longest moves on to the effort involved, which results in a burst blood-vessel in his temple and consequent haemorrhage, while the third repeats this and stresses the pain. This is the injury, self-inflicted, from which Roland will die: no Saracen wound is, or can be (cf. ll.2152-54), involved. That it should be the action which at first he had rejected which kills him is highly significant for the interpretation of his change of heart: it is wholehearted reparation for his earlier decision which leads to Roland's apotheosis and makes him worthy of it.

The three laisses use a sort of 'cross-cutting' (in cinemato-graphic terms; or, prefiguring later romances, *entrelacement*) between Roland and the main army (the sound of whose trumpets clearly cannot reach Roncevaux, cf. ll.2103-14). They contain two further motifs: the King's comments on the sound and the reactions of others to them, and illustrate the technique of elaborating in subsequent laisses a motif introduced briefly in the first. Ganelon's one-line attempt (line 1760) to deny the inference drawn by Charles is developed in CXXXIV into a lengthy story, preceded by outrageous insults to the emperor (ll.1771-72), about Roland's taking of Noples (perhaps the subject of an independent poem); in CXXXV Ganelon's interventions are replaced by Naimon's identification of the traitor, so that the parallelism in the first two laisses accentuates the change in the third (see Rychner's *reprise bifurquée*, *138*, pp.80-86, and Chapter 4, pp.109, 112-13).

Laisses CXXXVI-CXXXIX

Apart from the last few lines of CXXXIX, these laisses recount the reaction of Charles and the army to the realisation that Roland is in distress. They are not precisely *laisses similaires*, but similar themes, with echo and variation, occur in each. The splendour of the host as it arms and rides back in the brightening evening (line 1807) is described in the usual terms of colour, reflected light and, in the fourth laisse, the sound of the bugles as they re-echo against the olifant (ll.1832-33); each laisse then moves to the anxious words exchanged among the men, in both direct and indirect speech, about Roland and his fate. There are important variations: expressions of hope are twice crushed with an authorial 'De ço qui calt?' followed by the flat warning that it is too late (ll.1806, 1840-41); in CXXXVII, the fears expressed about Roland lead Charles to order the arrest of Ganelon, who is handed over to the cooks for humiliating treatment. The simile comparing him to a chained bear (line 1827) picks up a motif running through the poem: ll.727, 732 (*ver(s)* probably scribal for *urs* in *O*), 2557-62, 3735-37; the packhorse he rides recalls that with which he threatened Marsile (line 481). In CXXXVIII, the description of the returning army is prefaced by a recall of the *Halt sunt li pui* motif (cf. ll.814-15, and p.45 above), which tends to be used at points of heightened tension; in the last laisse of the sequence, the army's anxiety about Roland is developed into a smooth transition (ll.1846-50) to the hero himself and the sixty splendid survivors with him.

Laisse CXL

(For detail on this key laisse and its significance, see van Emden, *157*.) Gazing at the hillsides strewn with the many Christian dead, Roland mourns for them, as a *guarant* must, and commends them into God's hands, in the *planctus* of ll.1854-62 (see Zumthor, *173*, pp.219-35, esp.232-33). This turns at line 1863 into words addressed also to the survivors, words which are of great significance for the interpretation of Roland's role, and which have been much discussed. One problem arises from the paratactic epic style: each of the six lines 1863-68 is a self-sufficient sentence, the absence of subordination making the passage difficult to interpret. The central issue is *pur mei*: *pur* can mean simply 'for', 'on behalf of', e.g. ll.807, 2937 (?), 3407, or 'in the name of', e.g. ll.82, 1177; but it can also have a stronger meaning, 'on account of', 'because of', as for example at ll.412, 686, 1063, 1075, 1241. If we see Roland as using this latter meaning here, then the speech is an admission of responsibility for the disaster.

Critics have tended to translate line 1863 in accordance with their general view of Roland; Short (*9*), for example, is quite consistent in using 'pour moi', though he scrupulously mentions both possibilities in n.1863. Short also adds 'et' in his translation of line 1864: 'et je ne peux ni vous défendre ni vous protéger', which tends to place the two lines on a footing of syntactic equality. I would argue (see *157*, p.37) that line 1864 is the explanation or amplification of line 1863, as the punctuation of the text (comma or colon after *murir*) in all editions known to me suggests. For *guarantir* means more than 'protéger' (see the discussion of *guarant* above, pp.53-54, and *157*, pp.37-45); and the role of *guarant* is what Roland accepted amid the plaudits of the French at line 1161, of which line 1864 is the sadly ironic echo. Roland has to admit that he can no longer fulfil this function, and that he must pass it to God, the ultimate *Guarant* (line 1865). This line seems to convey a bitter contrast between his failure and God's infallible help, and the next reinforces the impression. 'Oliver frere, vos ne doi jo faillir' has an order of words in the second hemistich which is marked, and stresses the *vos* (two-thirds of similar constructions in the poem, on a rough count, have the object pronoun after the finite verb). In these circumstances, I believe *pur mei* at line 1863 has the stronger meaning 'because of me', amplified and justified by the next three lines.

Laisses CXLI-CXLIV

The last two lines of CXL express Roland's pain and determination to continue to fight to the death, and we see this put into effect in the next laisses. Roland's furious, vengeful (line 1873) assault and its results are related in CXLI, the flight of the Saracens before him being described in a striking epic simile (ll.1874-75) and commented on by Turpin, with a famous expression of the prelate's preference for the warrior (the *bellator*) over the conventionally superior *orator* or man of prayer, the monk (ll.1876-82). The Christians continue to diminish in number (line 1885), in spite of their desperate defence as men who know no prisoners will be taken (ll.1886-88). It is now that Marsile kills three more of the Peers (ll.1895-96), as well as Bevon, who does not belong to that group. With a curse and a grim, verbally effective threat (ll.1900-01; swords often had their name written on the blade), Roland avenges his friends by cutting off the Saracen's right hand, which counterbalances himself seen as Charlemagne's right arm (ll.597, 720-27, 1195). He also kills Marsile's son; this causes 100,000 to flee, but again the author, increasing the sense of tragic inevitability, kills all optimism with the formula 'De ço qui calt?' at the head of the next laisse.

There is indeed still Marsile's uncle Marganices, the caliph whose presence among the hostages Charles had demanded as retribution for Basan and Basile (ll.488-94), whom Ganelon had saved with his lies (ll.681-91), and who leads 50,000 Africans against the handful of French. Roland calmly states his certainty that death is imminent, the *or* of line 1923, line 1935 suggesting that only now does he really accept what Oliver has grasped all along. He uses the realisation, with echo across two laisses (ll.1922-37), to encourage the survivors to uphold their reputations and that of France, receiving enthusiastic support from Oliver and the others.

Laisses CXLV-CXLIX

Oliver's exclamation (line 1938) is his first intervention since the Horn Scene, and leads into his very moving death-scene. Marganices strikes him a terrible but cowardly blow in the back with his spear, and, in triumphing over him, valorises Oliver for us: 'Kar de vos sul ai ben vengét les noz'. Oliver cannot be defeated fairly, and he kills his attacker, refuting his accusations against Charlemagne (ll.1958-63; cf. pp.55-56 above) before calling Roland to his aid. CXLVII shows him avenging himself insatiably (line 1966) while strength remains, the author giving an impression of frenzied but effective violence by his indiscriminate cutting through limbs and equipment, ll.1968-69, followed by the heaping up of dismembered bodies. Those who argue that Oliver cancels his *compagnonnage* with Roland at the Second Horn Scene (line 1735) should note the future tenses in lines 1736 and 1977: only death can part them.

In CXLVIII-CXLIX Roland's grief causes him, in the hyperbolic epic way, to faint, and this leads to one of the most moving moments in the poem: Oliver, blinded by loss of blood so that he cannot recognise any man, continues the frenzy of killing seen in CXLVII by striking Roland a terrible blow on the helmet. Critics who wish to depreciate Oliver in favour of Roland have made much symbolical, even allegorical hay with this fact (e.g. Brault, *7*, pp.227-29; Pensom, *127*, pp.155-57; Cook, *50*, p.96). I do not believe that the poet's presentation of Oliver's role in the battle and in the decision-taking supports any view which exploits his condition as symbolising spiritual blindness. Nor do I believe that the exegetical level of allegory, as applied in mediaeval biblical and didactic studies, is generally appropriate to *chansons de geste* (see Chapter 4, p.120).

It is significant that Roland, in the state of mind shown in CXL, is able to conceive of the possibility that Oliver might have struck him deliberately: though puzzled (line 2002) by the absence of the obligatory *desfi*, he has clearly accepted his friend's indignation as expressed in the Second Horn Scene, and is affected by it. From the moment of his regrets for his men in CXL, in fact, he increasingly shows a new gentleness, now expressed in his question (ll.1999-2002, though cf. already ll.1162-64). The reply is very moving: in line 2004, the poet, using chiasmus (see Chapter 4, p.121), links Oliver's inability to see Roland with a prayer to the Lord God to look protectively on him; pardon asked for is at once given, here and before God (ll.2005-07), and, with an understated dignity which is a masterstroke of affective writing, the love of the two heroes is expressed in a formal bow, even as they are parted (ll.2008-09).

Laisses CL-CLI

The death of Oliver is that of a Christian of the early twelfth century (before individual confession to, and absolution from, a priest was seen as the indispensable condition of salvation) with an audible and general *mea culpa* (line 2014) which does not specify particular sins (Brault, *7*, p.230, Payen, *126*, pp.111-16). His last thought goes to Roland. Oliver dies face down (line 2025; an attitude of contrition), gently mourned by Roland, who faints again in his sorrow, his stirrups preventing a fall. The repetition of 'Oliver sent' at ll.1952, 1965 is to be compared with the much heavier structural use of echo in Roland's death scene (see pp.71-74 below): each dies a hero's death, but there is a clear gradation.

Laisses CLII-CLXI

The end of the battle takes nearly another 150 lines, even though during Roland's faint all the remaining Franks die except Turpin and Gautier del Hum, who returns from his position on the upper slopes (see ll.803-13), having lost his men, because he wants to die near Roland. He exists, like Aude later, only to valorise Roland by his moving words (ll.2045-53); his return does not affect the narrative, for he dies almost immediately (line 2076) as the Saracens, afraid to approach (line 2073) hurl throwing-weapons (considered unchivalric and cowardly) at the trio of survivors. (For the commonly accepted view that a laisse, present in all other witnesses except the *Karlamagnús saga*, is missing between CLII and CLIII, see Bédier, *32*, pp.189-92, Hemmings, *1*, n.2055. Segre, *6*, pp.267-69 gives a balanced assessment. My own opinion coincides with Horrent, *84*, pp.173-77 and – though for other reasons – Hecht, *77*, pp.73-76: the extra dialogue is otiose, and was probably inserted in the archetype of the non-*O* manuscripts.)

The wounding of Turpin and the death of his horse under him afford the poet two fine moments: the Archbishop's proud refusal to be beaten and his epic counter-attack on the enemy (ll.2085-98), and Roland's offer to dismount alongside him (ll.2138-43). The latter emphasises the courtesy of the hero quite gratuitously, since Viellantif too is killed under him before he can do so (ll.2160-61). All this is inserted into an account of the heroism of Turpin and Roland (ll.2089-98 – see *1*, n.2095 —, 2099, 2122-33, 2142-43) and of the growing disarray of the Saracens (ll.2060-65, 2071-73, 2113-19, 2146-54), as a prelude to their flight (ll.2162-65). This is caused by the sound of the returning army's trumpets, responding at last audibly to the final and feeble sounding of the olifant by Roland, now gravely weakened by his self-inflicted wound (ll.2100-02, cf. ll.1753-87).

As the Saracens flee, terrified by the prospect of facing Charlemagne and his army, Roland, unable, because unhorsed, to pursue them, tends the Archbishop's wounds. His request for leave to find the other Peers' bodies and to bring them to the prelate for blessing and absolution (cf. line 2205) leads to Turpin's thrilling affirmation of victory: 'Cist camp est vostre, mercit Deu, [vostre e] mien' (Samaran, *140*, p.47, reads *vostre e* under an erasure in this line; cf. for a contrary view Segre, *6*, p.285). They are the last two living persons on the field and the enemy has fled: it is a victory, not a defeat. But Roland owes this victory to his recalling of Charlemagne (ll.2113-19, 2146-54); it is obtained only at the price of reversing his first decision.

Laisses CLXII-CLXVII

The death of the Archbishop now follows over six laisses, interspersed with Roland's quest for the bodies of the Peers and his grief over the body of Oliver, and brought about by Turpin's dying efforts to help the hero. There are three Peers missing from the list at ll.2186-2201; it is probable that there are lines omitted in *O* here (Segre, *6*, p.286). Oliver's corpse makes a climax in laisse CLXIII, and is the cue for a new *planctus* from Roland, whose praise of his friend's valour is generous and implies a new humility (line 2214). It is no doubt to some extent inherent in the changed situation, but it is noticeable that, once he decides to sound the horn, Roland exhibits the Christian virtues of humility and charity, and uses specifically Christian language (e.g. ll.1854-56, 1865, 2252-58, 2344-50), more explicitly than before that point, though by no means to the exclusion of the feudal.

Turpin's death arises from the same virtue of Christian charity: seeing Roland unconscious, he tries to fetch water for him, the poet describing his touchingly unsteady steps and his fall (ll.2225-32); the next laisses relate his death, followed first by high praise from the author (ll.2242-45), then from Roland in his *planctus*. The attitude in which Turpin dies, with hands crossed on his breast (line 2250), rather than joined (cf. line 2240), is unusual and signifies firm faith in the saving power of the Cross (P. Ménard, quoted by Short, *9*, n.2249).

Laisses CLXVIII-CLXXVI

The death of Roland takes up nine laisses, divided into three groups of three, in which repetition of 'Ço sent Rollant' (ll.2259, 2284, 2297, 2355, 2366) measures the approach of death, framing the attempt to break Durendal, with its repetition of *ferir* (ll.2301, 2312, 2338). The art with which the third group, in particular, is constructed will be analysed in Chapter 4, pp.116-17; I concentrate here on the thematics of the series. The first group explains the content of the second by recounting how a Saracen, feigning death among the bodies (ll.2275-76) attempts to steal Durendal from the apparently dead hero. The opening lines, with their precise (if unscientific) description of the mortal injury (ll.2259-60, cf. ll.1763-64, 1785-86) stress again that Roland dies from his own efforts in blowing the olifant, not from enemy blows. His action in going a crossbow-shot towards Spain is explained later (ll.2361-63, 2863-67): it is his symbolic claim to having died a conqueror, though, once again, the victory is pyrrhic and due to his change of heart about recalling Charles. The importance of such symbolism explains the Saracen's seizing Durendal (ll.2281-83) and Roland's reaction to the event, once he has killed the thief and scorned the theft (ll.2287-94).

In the next series of three laisses, we witness the famous scene of the unavailing attempt to break Durendal on the dark-coloured stone. The physical action, retained even in the very different text of the *Pseudo-Turpin* (and therefore in the Charlemagne window in Chartres Cathedral), is repeated in each of laisses CLXXI-CLXXIII, but with different information in each case. First (ll.2303-11) we learn of Roland's regrets for his sword because of the many battles in which he has used it and his fear of its falling into unworthy hands. This is expanded in a significant way in CLXXII, where we hear that the sword was given him by Charles at the command of an angel sent by God (ll.2318-21), so that it is a divinely given responsibility. Roland then rehearses his victories again (cf. ll.197-200), in a new and longer list, and with a changed emphasis. Now each place-name is prefaced by 'Jo l'en cunquis': he has conquered *with* the God-given sword *for* Charlemagne. Again there is the fear, now prayerfully expressed in a synthesis of the Christian and the temporal, that Durendal might be captured by a Saracen (ll.2335-37). Here at last the sacred and the feudal come explicitly together; there is indeed no conflict between them (Boatner, *35*), but, before the Second Horn Scene, Roland's language had largely been at the feudal pole of the axis. The third laisse in the group ends with another such synthesis (ll.2349-54) and completes our understanding of Durendal's significance: it is *seintisme*, containing important relics (ll.2344-48, cf. Murgleis, Ganelon's sword, line 607). The Christian elements of the narrative are certainly becoming more insistent.

The death itself now takes place in the final group, a series of *laisses similaires* of the 'dynamic' kind, in which motifs develop or reduce, advancing the narrative rather like incoming tidal waves on the shore. In CLXXIV, the stress is on Roland's choice of the place of his death: a hint of a *locus amoenus* (ll.2357-58), in which he protects sword and olifant beneath his body. He claims his status as victor by turning his face to the enemy land (ll.2360-63, cf. line 2866 and p.72 above; certainly, he never forgets the matter of reputation, even as the sacred becomes more insistent, but they now exist in synthesis) and says his *mea culpa*, proffering his glove to God. These latter motifs are much expanded in the succeeding laisses: in the third, the *mea culpa* is preceded by a meditation on his life of conquest, sweet France, his family and his earthly lord, Charlemagne. On the significance of the glove, see Brault (*7*, pp.255-60), with a useful discussion and references, especially to the contributions by Faith Lyons (*107*) and W. Mary Hackett (*76*), showing that the proffer of a glove is commonly associated with repentance. It thus fits in well with the *mea culpa*, which, like Oliver's, is not specific (cf. p.69 above, and Brault, *7*, p.230, Payen, *126*, pp.111-16). One need not necessarily follow Brault in excluding the possibility of a simultaneous feudal symbolism, in which the glove may also represent Roland's life, returned like a fief to the feudal lord when the holder can no longer defend it (cf., though in contrasting circumstances, the gesture of Marsile, ll.2830-34, where the feudal point is clear).

In CLXXVI, the *mea culpa* is extended into a short prayer, resembling a litany or prayers used in the hour of death, of a type known as the *credo épique* or *prière du plus grand péril* (cf. ll.3100-09; see Labande, *99*, in whose classification these are *prières embryonnaires* (p.62), there being many much longer ones in later poems). The angels, who are first mentioned as the final motif in the second laisse of the three, are now named; it is important to note that the angel 'Cherubin' evokes, not the baroque cherubs more familiar today, but a powerful figure with four great wings of blue and silver; Saint Michael has here (and at ll.152, 1428) the emotive title, *du Péril (de la Mer)*, associated with the Saint's cult at the Mont Saint Michel, suggesting now protection for the soul as it crosses the waters of death.

The bearing of the count's soul to Paradise (line 2396) by the mighty angels is a fitting climax to the role of Roland in the poem, for he dies as a saint of the Church as well as a conqueror. That sanctity, expressed in his direct entry into bliss, is that of the repentant sinner: he has confessed his sins in the general form of the *mea culpa*, but we have also seen that he has made a costly reversal of a decision taken under the influence of what may be called a tragic error, a *hamartia*, and in that sense also he may be seen as having repented. It is by that repentance that he becomes worthy of his apotheosis, which in turn, of course, removes the poem from the realms of tragedy and moves it into the pattern of a Saint's Life, in which the value of the Saint's sacrifice is often shown in a lengthy sequel. That sequel is mainly the Baligant Episode, which we must examine in the next chapter, starting with Charlemagne's return and destruction of the rest of Marsile's army, which strictly speaking is not part of the episode, but leads into it.

3. Interpretation: the aftermath

Before reaching the Baligant Episode proper, with its textual problems, we must deal with the immediate sequel to Roland's death: the arrival of Charlemagne in Roncevaux and his pursuit and slaughter of Marsile's remaining men.

Laisses CLXXVI-CLXXXIV

The poet wastes absolutely no time in continuing with the story. Laisse CLXXVII begins with one line of summary as a link, then Charles arrives, to find the slain everywhere. He calls desperately for his nephew, Oliver and the other Peers, as well as Turpin; the poet gives his speech, which is heavily anaphoric, the form of the classical topos *Ubi sunt?* (see *1*, n.2402). Only here do we have a full list of the Peers (ll.2402-10; omit Turpin). Their fate causes hyperbolic expressions of grief (ll.2414-22), including, significantly, Charlemagne's regret that he was not present at the start of the fighting (ll.2412-13), which may legitimately be interpreted as a further comment, given to one of the characters of the poem for the audience's benefit, on Roland's decision. The poet exploits Naimon's standard role as counsellor by having him point to the dust still being raised by the fleeing enemy, and urging Charles to vengeance; the value of the dead is then stressed through the precautions taken to guard their bodies (ll.2432-42), after which the pursuit is undertaken with a vigour which belies Ganelon's belief in the emperor's dependence on his 'right arm'.

Now follows (CLXXIX-CLXXX) the famous miracle of God's prolongation of daylight, inspired by that performed on behalf of Joshua in the Bible (Joshua X, 12-14; cf. *1*, n.2449): Charlemagne's mythic status as Priest-King, linked directly by angels to God (line 2452), is thus underlined again. The pagans are caught in the appropriately named and fictional *Val Tenebrus*, and their deaths are divided between the avenging swords and the deep waters of the non-fictional Ebro (line 2465), which might indeed be encountered, though at a great distance, by those fleeing from Roncesvalles to Saragossa. The horrors of drowning are given some emphasis (ll.2469-74) to stress the ineffectiveness of the pagan 'gods' (line 2468) and the extent of the vengeance, linked by line 2475 to the mourning for Roland.

The next four laisses show the Christians camping on the field of battle for the night; they have taken much booty (line 2478), but they are incapable of further effort. Here, indeed, the poet talks of the tiredness of the army (and its horses), but this is the only time that the army is described in the sort of terms implied by scholars who see the disaster as stemming from the battle-weariness of Charlemagne and his men; and this is physical, not mental, exhaustion, described in graphic terms (ll.2493-95, 2520-24) but dispelled by a night's rest (cf. Chapter 2, pp.24-25). The passage is notable too for a fictional explanation of the name of Charlemagne's sword *Joieuse*, so called for the joy procured by having the tip of the Holy Lance enshrined in the pommel of the sword; this in turn purports to explain the French warcry *Monjoie* (ll.2501-10). For a recent theory (one of several) on the real origin of *Monjoie*, see *9*, n.1181, cf. notes 2504, 3093; the historical fact that the Lance was claimed to have been discovered at Antioch in 1098, during the First Crusade, is a further link of the poem with the excitement of that heady period.

Laisses CLXXXV-CLXXXVI

The two dreams, visions inspired by the Archangel Gabriel (ll.2526-28), which succeed the four laisses just described, are to be read as a sequel to the two dreams preceding the loss of the rearguard (LVI-LVII; cf. Chapter 2, pp.41-42). Here, too, the first of the pair prefigures a coming battle (ll.2529-31), while the second refers to the punishment of Ganelon. The dream in CLXXXV is longer than the others, and differs by containing apocalyptic symbolism: Baligant, represented by the lion (line 2549), probably prefigures the Antichrist, surrounded by animals associated with the lion-mouthed beast of the Apocalypse (Revelation 13. 2; see Braet, *40*, pp.157-58, with further bibliographical references). The second dream of the pair seems to refer even more precisely than LVII to the trial preceding Ganelon's punishment, in that a *brohun* in chains (cf. ll.1827, 3735-37) is supported by thirty bears related to it (ll.2557-62; the meaning of *brohun* has been the subject of controversy: it is still translated *ourson* by Short, but see Braet, *39*, who considers that it designates a type of dog. From an incomplete review of occurrences, I suspect that *brohun* may mean 'cub' of either species, as required by the context).

The outcome of both combats is, as before, left deliberately in the air, line 2567 echoing line 2553, while line 2554 reproduces the 'unending nightmare' effect discussed in relation to LVI-LVII (Chapter 2, p.42); Charles however wakes at the end of the second dream, after which the narrative returns to Marsile in CLXXXVII. But the announcement of a second battle must surely be the consequence of the presence in the poem of the Baligant episode (to argue the contrary process, that the episode was suggested by the third dream, as does Duggan, *56*, leaves without convincing answer, *pace* Duggan pp.61-63, the obvious question: why announce a non-existent battle?). The question nevertheless remains: can the Baligant episode be accepted as 'authentic' or not?

I agree with Duggan that this adjective, about which much of the critical debate has turned, is misleading (*56*, pp.59-60). For representative critical views on the controversy, see: (for 'authenticity') Aebischer, *26*; Delbouille, *53*, pp.32-61; Le Gentil, *101*, pp.113-18; Brault, *7*, pp.270-71; Hunt, *86*, p.793; Hecht, *77*, pp.98-100; (against) Rychner, *138*, pp.38-40; Pidal, *130*, pp.123-29; Owen, *119*; Allen, *29*; Keller, *92* (since for Keller the episode is a late-comer among several layers of stratification). Like any other fictional narrative element, as distinct from the historical kernel of the subject, the episode, which occupies roughly laisses CLXXXVII-CCIII, CCXV-CCLXXII (a quarter of the poem), has been introduced at some stage in the evolution of the story. The question is, when? Certainly there is no trace of it in the (rather garbled?) summary of a version of the subject preserved in the *Nota Emilianense* (third quarter of the eleventh century; on this document, see especially R.N. Walpole, *170*). If Duggan is right to see in the episode the influence of the traumatic events surrounding the Battle of Mantzikert (1071; cf. Hunt, *87*, pp.210-11), Baligant would seem, from both indications, to date from about same period as our version.

Certain stylistic differences have been said to distinguish the Baligant episode from the rest of the poem. To take two mentioned by Duggan (*56*, p.60), the absence of *laisses similaires* in itself is not very convincing: the episode consists mainly of preparations for the battle and fighting, so that there is little scope for the use of this technique; by the same token, however, the absence of the epic blow which cleaves the opponent in two, common in Roland's battle, does appear significant. The late Alison Elliott (*63*) and I (*161*) have both shown how a *remanieur* may exhibit different formulaic preferences in passages where he is composing freely from those in which he is following a written source, even though reworking it; two written sources might similarly leave divergent traces.

It is certainly also true (and uncharacteristic of the *Roland* poet) that the intervention of Baligant is not prepared in the least before the dream in CLXXXV, and even there he is not named. Then we are suddenly told at ll.2609-21 that, in the first year of Charlemagne's seven-year campaign, Marsile had sent word to his overlord, the Emir Baligant in 'Babilonie' (Cairo), asking him to fulfil his feudal duty of protection to his vassal. Rather lamely, it may seem to us, the poet explains Baligant's delay by the distance and the time taken to summon his men and prepare their transport (ll.2622-27); now they arrive just in time to challenge Charlemagne.

Yet Ross G. Arthur (*30*) has pointed to an interesting parallel from a history of the First Crusade by Petrus Tudebodus, where there is no question of extraneous material being introduced into a story; a very similar conjuncture of events is described, and with a similarly abrupt transition in the narrative. The Crusaders, having taken Antioch and inflicted heavy casualties, were confronted two days later by a vast army, made up of many different Muslim peoples enlisted over 'a long period of time' and led by Kerbogha, summoned 'in the past' by the defeated Saracen commander of Antioch. Arthur concludes: 'the "some years before, letters had been sent [...]" device is a conventional way of connecting two pieces of narrative material, but not two texts.' In other words, our objection to the lack of preparation for Baligant's intervention *may* be anachronistic.

I am however perfectly prepared to see in the Baligant episode a development of the *Roland* subject, perhaps created or introduced by the *remanieur* (Turoldus?) to whom we owe the assonanced version represented today by the Digby manuscript and *V4*, as well as some of the adaptations into other languages. (I do not however join Duggan in seeing those versions which lack the episode, while otherwise following Digby closely, as preserving the simpler *Roland* which no doubt still existed in the late eleventh century; they seem more likely to have cut it independently for just the sort of reasons as make modern critics doubt its authenticity.) Baligant may quite conceivably have been inspired, as Duggan suggests, by the disaster of Mantzikert (1071), which William of Tyre, author of the most influential account of the First Crusade, saw 'as the decisive event which led to the rise of the crusading spirit in Western Europe' (*56*, p.67).

Whatever we believe about it, two things may be said. Firstly, it is not simply inserted mechanically into the assonanced *Roland*, as Owen implies in his translation by printing it in italics, and inviting readers just to leave it out. Someone has fitted the material into the poem as we have it, interlacing it with the return of Charlemagne (ll.2397-524, 2845-973) and making it part of the conception of *this* version (cf. Cook, *50*, pp.103-04, Le Gentil, *101*, pp.116-18). Secondly, the effect of its presence is to increase the Christian/Crusading content by setting Roland's death into the wider context of the cosmic struggle between Cross and Crescent. Because of it, Roland's death leads to the defeat of Charlemagne's equivalent at the imperial level, rather than just that of King Marsile. Vengeance is complete (line 3109): it is not only the Saracens of Spain who are converted or slain, but an enormous army representing Islam itself. Saints' Lives, too, tend to set the death of the saint in the context of the struggle of the whole Church Militant.

Laisses CLXXXVII-CCIII

It is in this lengthy transition passage that the introduction of
Baligant takes place. We start with the return to Saragossa of the
wounded Marsile and the reaction of his remaining men. It is
typical of the propagandistic side of the *chansons de geste* that
defeated Saracens take their disappointment out on the 'idols' of
their 'gods'; ll.2580-91 (cf. ll.2618-20, 2696-97; also ll.2468-70,
3490-93) are the earliest extant example of this motif, which is
connected with the 'ordeal-minded' conception of religious war as
being almost a trial by combat between the deities involved (van
Emden, *160*, Scully, *142*). Bramimunde as yet shows no sign of the
desire for conversion which will lead to her baptism at the very end
of the poem, though she joins in the condemnation of the 'gods'
who have failed their followers (ll.2600-01, 2714-18).

It is the queen who first refers explicitly to Baligant, by his
title of *li amiralz*, at line 2602; only in the next laisse do we learn
his name, together with the circumstances of his coming, discussed
above. The description of the great host sailing for Spain (ll.2630-
35) is another example of effective epic idealisation, by which even
the pagans' ships, ablaze with light, are not just impressive but add
to the *beauty* of the scene (compare ll.2635 and 1005, and Chapter
2, p.46; for a different reaction, see Brault, *7*, p.272; on the motif of
light in *Roland*, see Bennett, *34*). The motif of night turned to day
by the lamps and the carbuncle stones (a long-lived tradition insists
that gems shine with their own radiance) is repeated at ll.2643-44,
before day itself brings Baligant to land (ll.2646-47). Like Marsile
and Charles, the emir is seen in a *locus amoenus* setting (ll.2651-
54) surrounded by impressive numbers of kings and noblemen. His
arrogance is expressed in his first words (especially ll.2658-59); his
message to Marsile shows his confidence in his expectation, echoing
across a laisse frontier, of conquering all France (ll.2660-67). He
speaks as a feudal overlord come to fulfil his duty of protection to a
vassal (another example of the assumption that Saracen political
institutions resemble the French system). The scene dovetails
further with Roncevaux through the sending of the golden glove
which, he stresses with unconscious irony (line 2678), is for the

king's right hand, already lost to Roland's sword (line 1903; cf. ll.2700-01, 2719-20, 2795, 2829-30; the emphasis on this motif is one way of keeping Roland, as Charles's 'right arm' avenged by this wound, in our mind). Laisses CXCIV-CXCV stress the Saracens' hopelessness, which is confidently repudiated in the next laisse by the messenger, whose repetition of the intention to conquer all France elicits the information that Charles is still within easy reach (ll.2734-40), though Bramimunde's praise of Charlemagne sounds a pessimistic note. In CXCVII, we see the extent of Marsile's personal despair; Marsile, now without an heir and mortally wounded, very feudally offers Spain back to Baligant for its future defence. Nevertheless, the coming battle cannot be minimised: Marsile is confident in his lord's victory (ll.2742-51), and he returns the keys of Saragossa in token of his placing himself and the town in the emir's effective protection.

The next three stanzas serve largely to repeat and sum up the situation as seen by the Saracens, with emphasis on the death of Roland, Oliver, the Peers and the 20,000 by means of the messengers' report to Baligant. Epic poetry needs occasional summary, especially if it is intended for large and not necessarily attentive audiences and performed over more than one sitting; here the information also helps to further the process of dovetailing referred to above, since the emir is informed of events played out before his arrival. He is thereby encouraged to boast of speedy victory over a Charlemagne weakened by his loss (ll.2802-09). Such optimism obviously raises the stakes in the battle to come, for the audience.

In CCI, as the emir meets the grieving Bramimunde, her name is suddenly given as *Bramidonie* (line 2822), and remains so till the end of the poem. The change is not linked with the Baligant episode, since it is maintained beyond line 3681, while *Bramimunde* is still used at ll.2576, 2714, 2734. Nor is the new form supported by other versions (which suggest that the name ended in *-monde* throughout in the original); it is probably scribal, the result of the normal habit of abbreviating proper names. Marsile's grave state is dramatised by his calling of two Saracens to raise him to a sitting position, and the loss of his right hand stressed again by his use of the left (with overtones of bad omens connected with the 'sinister' side), in order to return his fief, symbolised by the glove, to his overlord. Baligant accepts with apparently sincere grief (line 2839) which is, however, brusquely expressed, for his impatience to catch up with Charles (ll.2836-37) must be made clear to the audience, as also in CCIII.

Laisses CCIV-CCXIV

The return of Charlemagne and his army to Roncevaux takes us back to the earlier story-line: whatever one's views on the status of Baligant, the bestowal of the bodies and the regrets of the king over them are clearly essential parts of Roland's story, if only to validate Turpin's reasoning at CXXXII. It is certainly fair to say that CCIV resumes precisely where CLXXXVI leaves off after the dream: the film-like 'cut' to Marsile in Saragossa which introduces Baligant, and which has its own time-scale, already including the next day (ll.2635-46, 2745, 2772, 2791), comes between the promise of waking in the morning (line 2569) and the actual dawn which recalls Charles to reality (ll.2845-46). The Archangel Gabriel, whom we left presiding over the king's visions, is still there and gives him a solemn blessing (ll.2847-48); and the poet has not forgotten that the night has been spent under arms (ll.2849-50, cf. 2498-501). The textual evidence does in principle suggest some editing-in of the intervening material, but, if so, it has been deliberate and careful, with skilful 'cross-cutting' from one location to the other. It resembles that used for relating the boasts of the pagan 'peers' (ll.848-1005) between the nomination of Roland to the rearguard and the first intimations of coming battle, though there the transitions take place within laisses, and are perhaps subtler (see Chapter 2, pp.45-47).

The haunting phrase 'En Rencesvals' (which also charac-terised the boasting scene just referred to) now echoes across the laisse-boundary at ll.2854-55 as Charles reaches the valley (note also the emotive, final simplicity of the second hemistich 'la o fut la bataille' in line 2854). Laisse CCV is used to explain again (cf. ll.2360-63) Roland's choice of the place of his death, further towards Spain than any other, the place of a victor. It is guided by Roland's prophecy about this and by the signs of his attempts to break Durendal (line 2875) that Charlemagne finds his nephew's body. After fainting for grief, the emperor speaks a long regret (*planctus*) over the body (CCVII-CCXI). These five laisses lack the symmetry of true *laisses similaires*, but they contain a great deal of echo as, between commending Roland to God's mercy (ll.2887, 2898-99, then 2933-34), Charles contemplates the effects of his loss both on his own feelings and on the safety of France (see Zumthor's excellent analysis, *173*, pp.219-35, esp.221-23). Physical signs of grief, hyperbolic here as elsewhere, punctuate the words (ll.2891, 2906-08, 2930-32, 2943).

As when Charles first came to Roncevaux (ll.2398-424), one of his barons (this time Geoffrey of Anjou) has to call the emperor back to the practical necessities, and the bodies of all but Roland, Oliver and Turpin are given Christian burial; the three heroes' corpses are prepared, with great reverence, for transport to France. All this retrospectively endorses Turpin's reasons for encouraging Roland to sound the oliphant at the end of the Second Horn Scene (ll.1742-51).

Laisses CCXV-CCXIX

We return to the Baligant episode: as Charles is about to leave, the vanguard of the pagans appears with the same expressive suddenness (and use of the same verb *surdre*, line 2975) as when Marsile's forces 'rose up' (line 1448) to begin the second phase of the battle with the rearguard. The arrogant challenge Baligant's messengers deliver (ll.2978-81) fittingly echoes the tone of the emir's first words (ll.2658-59) and leads to the immediate arming of the Christians, beginning with the emperor (ll.2987-95); a first *eslais*, or morale-raising gallop follows (ll.2996-97; cf. Roland's at ll.1152-69, and others at ll.3165-71 – Baligant – and ll.3341-44 – Charlemagne again). The martial splendour of the 100,000 Christians is stressed as raising Charlemagne's morale and giving promise of vengeance for Roland's death (ll.3009-12).

This latter theme is prolonged in the next laisse, CCXIX, when Charles calls upon two unknown barons, Rabel and

Guineman, to take the places of Roland and Oliver, carrying 'the sword' (unnamed, but obviously Durendal) and the olifant and riding at the head of the army. There is something absurd about this appointment: we see the two open the battle successfully at ll.3348-68, and Guineman is killed at ll.3464-68, along with two equally obscure knights and Richard de Normandie, better-known, at least in later epics. That is all, except that 'he who sounds the olifant' is mentioned admiringly at line 3193 and the sound of the horn itself at ll.3119, 3302, 3310; Rabel disappears from the story and plays no part, for example, in the trial of Ganelon, where he might fittingly have been used in the judicial combat against Pinabel. We may legitimately wonder whether the total inadequacy of the chosen barons as replacements is not intentional: the very thought of replacing Roland and Oliver is palpably absurd, and to entertain it is to underline that they are irreplaceable.

Laisses CCXX-CCXXVII

The rest of CCXIX and laisses CCXX-CCXXVII are devoted to the setting up of the divisions (*escheles*) of the army and assigning their leaders. The roll-call of regions of origin evokes much of the Carolingian empire, far exceeding the bounds of early twelfth-century France, and thus links the audience with a past perceived as legendary (cf. Chapter 2, p.15). A curious feature is that the army thus set up totals the hyperbolic figure of 350,000 men, much greater than the 100,000 mentioned at line 3000 (cf. also line 3124), and that the numbers in each *eschele* rise gradually from 15,000 to 100,000. The numbers are clearly not meant to be looked at closely, but the poet emphasises, in a deliberate gradation, the military power of the Carolingian host as well as the far-flung places from which its members come. On the details concerning the oriflamme and its change of name (ll.3092-95) see Short (*9*, n.3093; cf., for an attempt, in my view unconvincing, at dating the poem from the mid-12th century on this passage, Keller, *92*, pp.54-59, cf. van Emden, *163*).

Laisses CCXXVIII-CCXXX

Fittingly for this stage of the poem, where the Christian values of the Crusade have come to the fore, Charles utters a *credo épique* (ll.3100-09) of the same kind as Roland's dying prayer (ll.2384-88, see Chapter 2, pp.73-74) before the battle, asking for God's mercy to allow him to avenge his nephew. The purpose is, however, partly to keep the latter before our eyes, and the separation of *nevold* from *Rollant* in line 3109 stresses the name, which is also at the assonance and the last word of the laisse, particularly strikingly (cf. ll.3120; 1437). The description of the emperor as he mounts and leads his army back towards Spain (line 3128) is remarkable for one detail: he, and the others in imitation of him, wear their beards outside their hauberks (ll.3122-24, cf. ll.1843, 3315-19), as, later, does Baligant (ll.3520-22); the gesture seems to be a means of self-identification as well as of defiance (cf. Augustine's *in barba virtus*, to which reference is made in the discussion of Zumthor's Liège paper, *173*). I am not aware of other examples of this motif. (For the equivalence of *brunie* and *halberc* implied here, see the convincing study of Knudson, *97*. Cf. Edge and Paddock, *61*, pp.9, 183.) CCXXX is used to transfer the action, by the report of the pagan vanguard when they see the Franks (not by sound as at ll.1005 and 2105-06), to the camp of the emir.

Laisses CCXXXI-CCXXXV

These laisses, in which the emir and his men arm for battle, serve to describe Baligant in some detail: his body (ll.3157-62) corresponds to the 'epic warrior' type, apart from the white (instead of fair) hair appropriate to his great age (cf. ll.2615-16, and Charlemagne's 200 years, XL-XLII). His courage is praised (line 3163) and the whole summed up in a famous epitome: 'Deus, quel baron, s'oüst chrestïentét!' It is obviously important for the interest of the narrative that Charlemagne's opposite number should be a formidable opponent, and his *eslais* (ll.3165-67) makes the pagans certain of victory. The introduction of his son Malpramis, who is also praised (line 3176), allows an exchange (ll.3178-99) expressing the emir's satisfaction that Roland, Oliver, the Peers and the 20,000 are dead, and going on to state, somewhat paradoxically, that he is not afraid of the remainder (line 3189) but that they will fight well, encouraged by the olifant (ll.3190-99). CCXXXV is used to reward with a rich fief Malpramis's demand for the first blow (line 3200). He does not in fact strike it, since the poet gives it to Rabel (contrast Aelroth, ll.860-72, 1188-1212). This consequently gratuitous investiture gives the opportunity for a characteristically premonitory *fin de laisse* (ll.3212-13), stressing that he will not live to take possession.

Laisses CCXXXVI-CCXL

This passage describes the setting up of thirty Saracen divisions, so that the Christians will be outnumbered three to one. The proper nouns employed include authentic and fantasy names which are not more exotic, let alone grotesque, than those used in the first part of the poem; they no doubt intrigued the audience with their mysterious sound, in contrast to the familiar names associated with the Frankish *escheles* earlier. What is perhaps different, though only relatively, is the emphasis on ugly and peculiar characteristics (ll.3221-23, 3238, 3247-50, 3253, 3285, 3526-27); the *buisine*, a trumpet whose name derives from the Latin BUCCINA, is restricted to Saracens throughout (ll.1468, 3138, 3263, 3523); their *taburs* (ll.852, 3137) appear to refer to the fear inspired by these instruments in the Battle of Zalaca, 1086, and this indication has been used to date the poem (Le Gentil, *101*, p.31).

Laisses CCXLI-CCXLV

The preparations for the battle consist largely of encouraging speeches by the leaders, and threats and counter-threats as the great armies come within sight of each other (ll.3291-94). We learn about the standards (ll.3266-68) and the war-cry, *Precïuse*, after the name of Baligant's battle-flag; this is also the name of his sword, as no doubt the missing line(s) after line 3145 made clear (cf. line 3471, and the relationship between Charlemagne's sword *Joiuse* and the banner and battle-cry *Monjoie*). The threats end with Charlemagne's *eslais*, which leads straight into the fighting (ll.3341-44).

Laisses CCXLVI-CCLXIX

The first part of the battle lasts some 160 lines; after the two victorious single combats of Rabel and Guineman, followed by comments from the French rather than the combatants, the fighting is at first more general, less based on one-to-one combats than the opening of Roland's battle, with interjections from first Baligant (ll.3373-78, 3391-92, 3396-99), then from Charles (ll.3405-13). Both promise tangible rewards for their men, but the emperor also stresses the need to avenge the dead of Rencesvals, thus keeping the first battle strongly in the forefront of the audience's minds. His claim to be in the right against the pagans (line 3413; cf. Roland's similar sayings at ll.1015, 1212) is in the singular and, preceded by the call for vengeance for those killed at Roncevaux (ll.3411-12), again implies a personal grievance to do with the treachery committed by the enemy rather than a general religious statement (contrast perhaps line 3554 and cf. Chapter 2, p.47).

The next four laisses (CCLIII-CCLVI) slow down to concentrate on an episode affecting an individual: Naimon kills Malpramis, but is then attacked in his turn by Canabeus, the emir's brother, has much the worst of it and is in danger of death (ll.3432-42). This allows Charles to exercise his function as a *guarant* by killing Canabeus and taking Naimon into his personal protection (ll.3455-60). The emir kills Guineman and others (ll.3463-70); he is not yet aware of his son's death, and the news will precipitate his portentous question to Jangleu (CCLX). One can see why the poet could not allow Malpramis to be killed, like Aelroth, in the first encounter (contrast ll.1188-1212); making him ask for the privilege of the first blow would seem to be connected with the desire for a premonitory laisse-end (see above), but does leave an inconsistency.

A more general phase of fighting returns at line 3473, both sides suffering heavy losses. The emir's apostrophe to his gods (ll.3490-93) is not necessarily unfinished, as Whitehead's line of dots and comment suggest (see Hemming, *1*, n.3494: Bédier, *32*, p.176, does not, as is implied, support the hypothesis of an omission); with the substitution of *vos* for scribal *tes*, it is very much in the tradition of epic pagans' attitude to their divinities (cf. p.80

above). At all events, the call to the gods has a grave sequel: Baligant learns of the deaths of both son and brother at the hands of two Franks, one of whom is the emperor. In his deep grief, Baligant calls on his confidant, Jangleu, whose cognomen 'l'ultremarin' adds an overtone of mystery and exoticism at the end of the laisse.

Laisse CCLX

In this laisse, we have one of the high points of the episode: Baligant's question as to the outcome of the day sets him up, rather like Roland at ll.1722-23 (see Chapter 2, p.63), for a shatteringly direct and simple reply: 'Morz estes, Baligant'. His gods cannot help him against Charlemagne, but it is better to call his troops for a final assault, for the inevitable must not be delayed: 'Ço que estre en deit, ne l'alez demurant' is another of the lapidary last lines of a laisse which so characterise our poet.

Laisses CCLXI-CCLXIII

A short passage separates the prophecy from its fulfilment: stoically and defiantly the emir shows his white beard for identification (ll.3520-22; cf. p.85 above) and sounds a bugle to rally his men. The resultant terrifying attack by pagans described in animalistic terms and causing many Christian deaths is used to underline again Charlemagne's role as *guarant* of his men, by dramatic means: Ogier and others issue a challenge to him to avenge this shame (ll.3537-39), to which he responds by taciturnly leading the counter-attack. Ogier's bringing down of Baligant's standard-bearer and the banner and dragon-emblem he carries is of course a symbolic victory (cf. Brault, 7, p.308, though the main point is simply the loss of the banner which visibly represents commander and cause. On this passage, see Segre, 6, notes 3546-48, 3550, 3551; there may be some corruption in *O* here). Baligant realises that he is in the wrong against Charles (line 3554); in the context of line 3552, with its reference to 'l'estandart Mahumet', this is possibly a religious judgement (contrast ll.3413, 3592; 1015, 1212). The pagans lose morale (ll.3553-55), while the Franks' spirits rise.

Laisses CCLXIV-CCLXVIII

This adumbration of defeat, clear to those living in an 'ordeal-minded age' (cf. Chapter 2, pp.55-56), now leads into the climactic meeting of the commanders, perhaps symbolically in the middle of the field (line 3567). Their duel, too, partakes of the *judicium Dei*, the validity of both religions being at stake. The course of the fight is very like that of the formal judicial combat fought later between Thierri and Pinabel (ll.3873-930). The initial charge with lances couched results in both men being thrown from their horses, unwounded, by the breaking of the saddle girths and the slipping of their saddles (ll.3568-74, cf. ll.3878-81), which is followed by their jumping to their feet and continuing the fight with swords (ll.3575-86, cf. ll.3883-89). This phase of the combat, here (differently from the later fight) recounted across a laisse-boundary, includes the memorable premonitory line 3578: 'Seinz hume mort ne poet estre achevee' (cf. line 3914). It involves the description of great blows sending sparks flying (line 3586, cf. ll.3912, 3917) and a further premonitory *fin de laisse*, this time expanded to two lines (ll.3587-88).

Laisse CCLXVI brings an element which will become common in combats between representatives of different religions or lordships in later epics: both combatants try to persuade the opponent to make peace by offers of reconciliation and the promise of some future social position, or by calling upon him to convert to the other's religion. Both types are represented here: Baligant's offer is little more than a call to surrender in return for riches and security as his vassal, but Charles offers reconciliation if Baligant will only embrace Christianity (cf. ll.3892-909). Neither of course accepts, and the battle continues to its appointed end: there is first a great blow from the combatant destined to lose, which very nearly kills the ultimate winner (ll.3602-08; cf. ll.3915-22); in the case of Charles, the protection of God (line 3609, cf. line 3923) is mediated by the presence of the Archangel Gabriel at his side, with the famous encouragement at the end of laisse CCLXXVII: 'Reis magnes, que fais tu?' Reacting to both blow and supernatural support, as Thierri will later react (ll.3612-14, cf. ll.3924-25),

Charles now strikes the fàtal stroke which fulfils Jangleu's prophecy (ll.3615-19, cf. ll.3926-30), and shouts 'Munjoie' in triumph. The flight of the Saracens (ll.3623, 3625) cannot of course have an echo in Thierri's case, but the close resemblance of the two combats, only the first of which is in the Baligant episode, is striking and, for what it is worth, argues the same poetic touch. The single combat motif does certainly become fairly stereotyped in later poems, but the slightly ridiculous detail of saddles which deposit the riders on the ground (as against horses which are killed) is not a standard part of the motif in other epics.

Laisses CCLIX-CCLXXII

The immediate sequel to Baligant's death is rapid and brutal: the Saracens flee (the motif is repeated across the laisse-boundary) and the Franks explicitly take vengeance (line 3627), which keeps the loss of the rearguard in the audience's mind. The vividly evoked pursuit in the dusty heat (ll.3633-34) moves the narrative to Saragossa, where Bramidonie, still calling on Mahomet, tells her husband of Baligant's death. Marsile's turning his face to the wall as he dies of grief is a biblical gesture of despair (II Kings 20. 2: Hezekiah's reaction to Isaiah's prophecy of death was surely in the poet's mind, as later in that of Thomas, *Tristan*, 25, Douce Fragment, line 1759). Baligant's soul is seized by demons, a fate often allotted to Saracens in epic, but perhaps sparsely enough elsewhere in *Roland* (ll.1268, 1553) to be impressive here, at the end of the laisse, as the fitting punishment of a treacherous enemy.

Another memorable last line (3657) sums up the capture of Saragossa (CCLXXI), and the sack of its *sinagoges* (!) and *mahumeries* (!), with the destruction of their 'idols', is equally expeditiously told. I have already signalled the ubiquitous propagandistic slanders on Islam: they are probably another sign of the Crusading enthusiasm engendered by the capture of Jerusalem in 1099. This event is paralleled also by the brutal choice of Baptism or death given to the captured Saracens (ll.3666-72; cf. *Gesta Francorum*, *18*, pp.91-92, where indeed the ferocity is even greater; this anonymous chronicle generally reflects very similar attitudes, values and beliefs about Islam to those of our poem). That the queen is taken captive to France to be converted by love (stressed at the end of the laisse, line 3674) contrasts with the more normal brutality in a way which makes the latter seem even worse (but we must beware of anachronistic judgements).

Laisse CCLXXIII

This long and somewhat heterogeneous laisse (see *1*, n.3675ff.) recounting the return to Aix-la-Chapelle brings the Baligant episode to an end (at line 3681 in Owen's translation). The account of the journey fulfils Turpin's hope of Christian burial, though first the olifant is deposited at Saint-Seurin in Bordeaux, where pilgrims could see it at the time of the poem's composition (line 3687); the bodies of the three paladins are buried at Saint-Romain in Blaye. These references to exploitations of the Roland legend at authentic churches in the Bordeaux area are of course central to Bédier's theory of pilgrimage routes, in this case to Compostela (*31*, III, pp.341-54, though Santiago is never mentioned in our poem).

Laisses CCLXXIV-CCLXXV

The death of Roland's betrothed Aude is placed between the announcement of Ganelon's trial at the end of CCLXXIII and its opening. The name has been heard only once before, when Oliver withdraws his permission for his comrade's marriage (line 1720). She does not figure among those Roland recalls at his death (as Hemming, *1*, n.3708ff.. says, this is a man's world). Yet the name causes no problems of recall. The scene of Aude's death is one of the celebrated high points of the poem, mainly because of its dignity and simplicity. Later versions were to develop it in a sentimental and sensational direction, with premonitory dreams and an invitation from her dead brother to join him and Roland in bliss. Our poet uses the death as another valorisation of the hero: offered the hand of the heir to the throne in place of Roland, she says simply that such a word is foreign to her: there is no meaning to life after his death, and she falls dead at Charlemagne's feet.

There is nothing sentimental here. The word 'amur' is not used, and it is more a matter of what is fitting: as perhaps with

Rabel and Guineman (see p.84 above), the point made is simply that Roland is irreplaceable. The emotion is consequently all the stronger, heightened by sober, solemn lines filled with affective overtones: ll.3709 (carrying an echo from Roland's death scene, cf. line 2320), 3717-19, 3723, 3726-27. The escort of four countesses who spend the night with the body accentuates Aude's worth, as does the rare honour of burial by the altar of the convent church. Such was the impact of this scene that, in later epics, Aude becomes 'la Belle Aude', with automatic preceding epithet, or even 'Bellaude'. Mercifully, not yet here: 'Alde la bele est a sa fin alee'.

Laisses CCLXXVI-CCXCIII

It is impossible to separate the trial of Ganelon from the judicial combat by which it is decided. Except where a person was captured red-handed, a mediaeval trial was normally settled by oaths tested by an ordeal (especially before the only partially successful condemnation of the institution by the Fourth Lateran Council in 1215). This was either unilateral (e.g. that by hot iron) or bilateral, the latter almost always a single combat, in which God was thought to give victory to the defender of the true oath. Able-bodied men generally fought for themselves, though women, priests and men who could plead *essoine*, 'necessity' based on sickness or old age, were represented by champions. One of the curious features of the present case is Ganelon's failure to fight himself; it may be that the author felt that death in combat would be insufficient punishment.

Here the oaths are the result of Charlemagne's attempt to make his vassals give judgement against Ganelon, an attempt which appears to fail. CCLXXVI reiterates the emperor's return to Aix (already mentioned before Aude's death, line 3706); there is no doubt an echo of the second and fourth dreams earlier (ll.726, 2556), which foretell the trial at Aix without hinting at the result. Ganelon's position, chained to a post and beaten by the serfs, hints at the 'bear' imagery which has accompanied the traitor throughout (see Chapter 2, p.66); the poet makes no pretence to impartiality (ll.3740, 3748). He emphasises the significance of the trial by invoking once more the *geste* as his prestigious source for the calling of vassals from many lands. Referring yet again to Aix-la-Chapelle and dating the event from the high feast day of Saint Sylvester (31 December), he shows Ganelon 'ki traïsun ad faite' dragged into Charlemagne's presence (ll.3742-49).

Laisse CCLXXVIII shows the emperor stating briefly the circumstances which he asks his barons to judge; the only element which is not self-evident to the audience is the accusation that Ganelon has betrayed for wealth (line 3756). I have argued that this, as the traitor's *primary* motivation, is not borne out by the narrative (see Chapter 2, p.37), but he certainly accepted presents (ll.515-19, 617-41), and his first reaction now shows that he is not uninterested in such matters. Hemming (*1*, n.3757) considers the reference to Roland's having got the better of Ganelon over some matter of property 'surprising', and so it is, in the sense that there has been no reference to this event. But I suggest that the poet is giving us a deliberately vague hint to account in part for the 'ancient hatred' that clearly exists between the men from (before) the beginning, and to remind us of that hatred, very opportunely, for it has brought about the events underlying the trial. Ganelon goes on to admit seeking Roland's death, but denies that this constitutes treason (ll.3759-60).

The next laisse explains this claim. After emphasising his splendid physique and the strength he draws from the presence of thirty members of his clan (a very pertinent reflection in contemporary terms, since the threat of vendetta – cf. ll.353-56 and Chapter 2, p.32 – is a very real one), the poet makes Ganelon set forth a superficially telling defence. He stresses his loyal service in Charles's host (ll.3769-70, cf. ll.3752ff.; we shall see that this circumstance in fact undermines the rest of his case), and claims that Roland took to hating him and therefore nominated him for a mission sure to end in death. He represents his own behaviour during the mission to Marsile as a clever manoeuvre to save his life (line 3774) and calls Charlemagne and his barons to witness that he had defied Roland, Oliver and their comrades publicly. The conclusion, that he has avenged himself, but that this is not treason, relies on the widely accepted notion of the legitimacy of inter-baronial warfare, which must be preceded by *diffidatio*, the formal *desfi* that he has indeed given (see ll.322-26, cf. Mickel, *110*, pp.44-45, 78-80).

The next two laisses introduce us to Pinabel, who emerges from the anonymous group of Ganelon's clan to answer the latter's plea for an effective defence: as a particularly respected warrior (ll.3782-85), he promises to fight in judicial combat any Frenchman who gives judgement in favour of a capital sentence. At first, in CCLXXXII-CCLXXXIII, it looks as if the threat is enough: when Charlemagne's vassals from all over the Empire withdraw to consider the judgement to be rendered, they are overawed by the physique of Pinabel (ll.3793-97; cf. Cook, *50*, p.120, n.148; Burgess, *46*). They cravenly agree that Ganelon should be freed and allowed to continue to serve Charles: the rationalisations of ll.3802-03, 3812-13 contrast tellingly with the real reason: no one wants to fight in the cause of justice (line 3804). The only dissentient, Tierri (line 3806), brother of Geifrei d'Anjou (who plays a quite large part in the Baligant episode), will deliver his own 'minority report' in the form of a challenge when the rest have spoken. Their words to Charles accurately reflect their deliberations: that the emperor can only accuse them of breach of feudal faith (line 3814), without overriding them, shows once more the effect of his determination to act in all matters by the advice of those of France (line 167) which underlay many of the early decisions, as we saw in Chapter 2 (pp.26, 28-29, 43).

As Charles laments his self-imposed inability to enforce his will, Tierri makes the judgement which he knows will be challenged by Pinabel. The poet stresses his slimness and average height (ll.3820-22) as against Pinabel's acknowledged size and strength (cf. ll.3785, 3797, 3839-40, 3885). There are overtones of David and Goliath here, for, as in the Old Testament, the Judgement of God will be made clearer by the physical inequality of the champions. Speaking like a good member of the court (*curteisement*) and claiming (as I understand the controversial line 3826) an ancestral right to give a judgement, Tierri exposes the flaw in Ganelon's claim to the right to private vengeance: whatever wrongs Roland might have done him, the fact that the former was doing feudal service to Charles at the material time means that the attack was not only betrayal towards Roland (line 3829) but above all treason and perjury towards the emperor himself (line 3830). The principle invoked here is well established in feudal custom: it is that of fidelity, as distinct from vassalage. While the latter involves the active service of the vassal (*auxilium et consilium*), the former enshrines the negative principle of not harming the lord's interests (see Dunbabin, *60*, pp.110, 232-34, Ganshof, *72*, pp.83-86, both quoting Fulbert of Chartres's letter to Guillaume V).

It is following this principle that Tierri passes the judgement that Ganelon deserves death and, clearly referring to Pinabel's promise to defend his kinsman against such a demand, he states his readiness to justify his ruling with the sword against any relation wishing to dispute it (ll.3834-36). Pinabel, his awesome power stressed by the poet (ll.3839-40), at once does so. A judicial combat thereby becomes inevitable, and Pinabel's handing over his glove is the normal pledge of attendance.

Much controversy has raged over the significance of the trial and combat for the dating, as well as interpretation, of the poem. While it is impossible to examine the issues involved in detail here, the matter may be followed up in Mickel's recent monograph (*110*), which gives a valuable review of the relevant scholarship, though his findings are controversial. Mickel convincingly refutes, in my view, the long-standing thesis of Ruggieri (*137*) that the details of the proceedings, as well as the brutality of the punishments, necessarily reflect a primitive Germanic stratum of an essentially oral tradition. On the other hand, Mickel's attempt to suggest a late date of composition, comparable with those of Mireaux (*111*) and Keller (*92*), mainly on the basis of what he sees as the influence of Roman Law on the account, fails to convince. Apart from the probable early date of the Digby manuscript (see Chapter 1, p.10), almost all Mickel's evidence for savage punishment for high treason, resulting from the application to treason of the Roman notion of *maiestas* under monarchs with theocratic pretensions, is thirteenth-century or later.

I see no problem in interpreting the events described on a feudal, rather than a theocratic, level. Not every detail can be precisely related to what we know of reality: for example, it was normal, until the middle of the twelfth century, to require the accused to produce oath-helpers or compurgators, who swore that they believed the defendant's oath to be true. In very serious cases, twelve oaths (defendant plus eleven compurgators) might be required; for the most serious accusations, multiples of twelve (Mickel, *110*, pp.123-29). Clearly, Ganelon's thirty *pleges* do not fit precisely into this calculation. In addition, though they appear to swear that he is loyal (?3847; the line is imperfect and controversial), the word *pleges* suggests that they are also guarantors against absconding (*110*, pp.119-22; contrary to Mickel's statement, Tierri has to find some too, line 3852). Finally, whichever function they have (and I agree with Mickel, p.127, that the poet has fused both roles; cf. van Emden, *160*, p.176), they are punished with a savagery not recorded in history (apart from some much later Spanish laws, see Duggan, *59*, pp.59-61), and paralleled only in *Huon de Bordeaux*, a late epic probably under the *Roland*'s influence (*59*, p.58).

I am not persuaded by Duggan's argument that the ferocity towards the *pleges* is an acknowledgement of the otherwise later, clerical, legend of Charlemagne's incestuous fathering of Roland: Duggan sees the exemplary punishment as reflecting the killing of the heir to the throne. There is no explicit hint of this legend in the *Roland*, and I find it implausible that such an extraordinarily oblique reference, or the allusion to St Giles at ll.2095-97 (*59*, p.63; cf. Mölk, *115*), would have satisfied an author wishing to exploit the incest for whatever reason. See in support Kullmann, *98*, pp.58-64.

The point surely is that all this is not fact, but fiction. There was real-life provision for the harsh punishment of compurgators of defendants subsequently proved guilty, though not (with the Spanish exceptions mentioned above) for their execution (Mickel, *110*, pp.125-26), and the poet no more strains the credulity of his hearers when he exaggerates the penalty, as a fitting measure of the unparalleled loss caused by Ganelon, than when he assures them that it is possible to cleave an armed knight from head to horse with a single sword-blow.

Mickel also clouds the issue when (p.44 *et passim*) he compares Ganelon's defence to modern 'plea-bargaining', and sees him as pleading 'guilty' to the 'lesser charge [of homicide], a charge which he seeks to portray as no crime at all' (ll.3757-60 are quoted in support). Ganelon does not plead guilty to anything: he admits killing but denies guilt by claiming his right to vengeance after due *diffidatio*, and it is with this defence that the intimidated barons agree (CCLXXXII). It remains for Tierri to point to the well-documented feudal restriction on Ganelon's right to private vengeance discussed above (pp.94-95), and to demand the due penalty.

It is by this means, too, that the poet side-steps the normal expectation that Ganelon would defend himself (though cf. also Nottarp, *117*, pp.298-99). Tierri is 'falsifying' a judgement made by his peers, so that it is open to anyone (line 3834) to challenge him; the duel thus takes place at one remove from the original charge. In this way, Ganelon is prevented from dying almost honourably in combat, and reserved for what may be historically unparalleled around 1100, but is a fittingly appalling end for a traitor whom Dante, in the same spirit, was to place, like Judas, in the bottom of the pit of Hell.

The preparation for the duel (CCLXXXV-CCLXXXVII) is certainly more detailed than similar scenes in most poems, and corresponds closely to the schema drawn up long ago by Pfeffer (*128*, pp.9-10, though there is a risk of circularity here; cf. also Nottarp, *117*, pp.269-93). The pattern of the combat, with its apostrophes to the opponent suggesting surrender on good terms, and the pattern of great blows leading to one almost fatal to the eventual winner (CCXCII), who replies with the decisive stroke, corresponds to that between Charles and Baligant (pp.89-90 above), and needs no further analysis. The cry for the execution of both Ganelon and his *pleges* comes unprompted – if somewhat inconsequentially! – from the Franks themselves (ll.3931-33).

Laisses CCXCIV-CCXCVI

The last lines of these laisses, which, like that of CCXCIII, all refer to the execution of the guilty, sum up their main business. After the rapturous gratitude expressed by Charles towards Tierri (ll.3939-40) and the return to the town, the killing begins. The Franks, here prompted by Charlemagne's question, reiterate the sentence of hanging on the thirty *pleges*. It is carried out at once; the stern resolve of the king is shown in the gratuitous threats to the executioner (ll.3954-55), and the grim, memorable last line (3959) underlines the fact that treason affects more people than the traitor himself, just as, indeed, Ganelon's actions had reached far more men than Roland, Oliver and the Twelve Peers whom he had defied.

There is some internal evidence suggesting that the same death awaited Ganelon in earlier versions of the poem: hanging is demanded by the barons at line 3932, but also prophesied by the poet at ll.1409-11. Quartering by horses is clearly more atrocious (even in executions of the fourteenth century, quartering was usually after death by other means). Ganelon's end may owe more to the fate of Discordia in the *Psychomachia* of Prudentius (see *110*, p.149; cf. also *3*, n.3963 for other examples, including Mettus in *Aeneid*, VIII, 642-45) than to contemporary judicial practice. That it is a question of literary imagination rather than, as Mickel argues (*110*, pp.145-49), a reflection of later forms of punishment influenced by Roman Law conceptions of *lèse-majesté* is suggested by the following condemnation of the eponymous hero in *Girart de Roussillon* (probably not earlier than 1170) for his plans to avenge himself on the king, his feudal lord, by murdering him. A holy hermit castigates this intention in *feudal*, not theocratic, terms, and the development of the motif of quartering here is very fictional, almost folkloric, rather than legalistic (I quote from the Modern French translation of this difficult text by Paul Meyer, *19*, p.238):

> " [...] et maintenant tu veux encore tuer *ton seigneur direct* ! [my emphasis] Mais alors tu ne trouveras plus clerc, ni saint homme, ni évêque, ni pape, ni docteur, qui consente jamais à te donner pénitence! La théologie

> et les auteurs nous montrent dans la loi du Rédempteur
> quelle justice on doit faire d'un traître. On doit
> l'écarteler avec des chevaux, le brûler sur le bûcher, et
> là où sa cendre tombe, il ne croît plus d'herbe, et le
> labeur y reste inutile; les arbres, la verdure y dépér-
> issent."

The fate of Ganelon, like this condemnation (which was probably influenced by it), is surely above all an exemplary punishment to fit an unparalleled crime in a work of literature. The pain suffered by the traitor is described with some relish (ll.3969-73), and the final line grimly echoes that of the previous laisse in denouncing treachery as beyond mercy.

Laisse CCXCVII

The Baptism of Bramimunde/Bramidonie, after proper instruction (ll.3979-80), fittingly crowns the conversion of Spain, over which she had reigned as Marsile's wife. It brings the poem, and the seven-year Spanish 'Crusade' it describes, to a satisfying conclusion. Brault (*7*, pp.334-35, with reference to Bédier, *32*, p.320), and others have plausibly explained the choice of her Christian name: the devil-beating Saint Juliana of Cumae, venerated at the eponymous Santillana del Mar in Asturias, though one wonders why Saint Sylvester's day, rather than her feast (16 February), was chosen for the final events of the epic (*pace* Brault's tortuous argument on this point). One may also wonder how many female Saints' names provide the right assonance . . . , but it would be fair to retort that the assonance of the laisse may have been chosen with Juliana in mind. This Saint, as Brault shows, had a sufficiently high profile in hagiography to make the choice an appropriate one on which to end the epic on a high Christian note, thus once more valorising implicitly the death of the hero. D.W. Robertson (*135*, pp.167-69) sees her conversion as 'Charlemagne's crowning achievement'.

Laisse CCXCVIII

Only the epic does not end at once. The final laisse opens up the vision of the never-ending Crusade, to which Charles, weary, drained and unwilling, is called by the Archangel. The identity of 'Reis Vivien' and the places mentioned have been debated, but, to my knowledge, without any convincing answers. And it does not matter: indeed, the mysterious names give a necessary, representative, generality to the call. The point is, we have no doubt at all that, in spite of his tears, Charlemagne will rise to the challenge.

The last line has also been the subject of endless discussion, as almost every word in it is capable of more than one interpretation. Who is Turoldus, with his very Norman name, and what is his function? Is he the poet, the singer, the scribe, or the author of the (alleged?) source? Is *geste* used in the sense which it has several times in the poem (though cf. line 3181), a presumably Latin *Gesta* (*Francorum*), or in one of the ways the word is used in later *chansons de 'geste'*, including simply 'story'? What is the meaning of *declinet*? The best attested meaning of this verb elsewhere, involving seeing *que* as the conjunction 'for', is perhaps the one first suggested by Jenkins, *3*, n.4002: 'is becoming infirm'. For recent comment, see Short, *9*, n.4002 and Cortès, *10*, pp.147-51. For my part, I will risk an aesthetically motivated preference. It involves interpreting *declinet* in a meaning it cannot clearly be shown to have elsewhere in Old French, though it might be an extension of the Latin meaning 'to decline (a verb)'. Since it provides an emotionally satisfying, because simple and *un*emotional, leave-taking by the author *or* singer, and recognising that the last line is yet another of the many aspects of *La Chanson de Roland* which are open to differing interpretations, I would happily go back to the translation of many of the earliest commentators:

Here ends the story that Turoldus tells.

4. Poetic Craft and Technique

Perhaps the most important feature of the style of *La Chanson de Roland* is its essentially dramatic nature, even though epic is a narrative genre (and our poem largely follows the usual straightforward linear storyline). We learn about the people in the story out of their own and others' mouths, and by their actions. The author makes character judgements in person only occasionally, and hardly at all at morally crucial moments (see e.g. ll.24-26, 231 and 775, both on Naimon, 674 and 844, both on Ganelon, 886-87, 895-99, 910, 1311-12, 2242-44, 3531-32, 3784-85, etc. as against ll.1093-97, where crucial issues are being debated); at ll.751-52 and 761-62 he offers an adverbial phrase and an adverb respectively to introduce Roland's reactions to Ganelon's action in nominating him; but we could supply them ourselves once we hear the words used by the hero.

It is because we find ourselves almost in the same situation as in the theatre, where we have to judge people from their words, demeanour and actions on the stage (though in the case of epic without the visual element), that there are legitimate differences of interpretation about the moral conception of our poem. Of course, the situation in the theatre is at its purest with a brand-new play, where we have no preconceptions about the characters; when we go to see a well-known piece by Shakespeare, say, we know what to expect from Henry V or Macbeth (if not Hamlet). It may well be that we are at a disadvantage in lacking the mediaeval audience's pre-knowledge of Roland and Oliver (for the use of the two names by eleventh and twelfth-century parents for their sons, see Lejeune, *103*, Aebischer, articles in *27, 28*; van Emden, *156*, with further bibliography on this subject; for an examination of the reception of the Roland character in other mediaeval works, which points interestingly, in the majority of cases, to views resembling the analysis in this book, see van Emden, *165, 166*, though cf. Mölk, *115*, pp.304-05).

Be that as it may, the method of exposition employed has implications for the texture of the narrative. Overall, I calculate that almost exactly 40% of the text consists of direct speech. This does of course include elements other than dramatic confrontation: there are regrets (*planctus*, see Zumthor, *173*, pp.219-35), one at least very long (ll.2887-943); there are also summaries of events (ll.2741-61, 2771-801) or prophecies of what is to happen (ll.2598-608, 3513-19) spoken by characters. But much of the direct speech is used to present the moral problems facing the heroes, and often, as we have seen, in the form of passionate argument. This technique is not by any means unique to the *Roland*: council scenes are included in many epics. For example, *Girart de Roussillon* (whose hero is one of the Twelve Peers in our poem) has a particularly solemn moral message about civil war, and makes enormous use of councils and *ambassades* in order to rehearse in depth the ethical issues involved.

A similar need to examine the moral choices and, by implication, the characters of the heroes of the *Roland* explains the great use of exposition by dialogue and argument, both in formal councils and between individual protagonists. The result in terms of narrative texture is uneven, and might among other things be used, superficially, to argue the adventitious nature of the Baligant episode. The main part of the episode (ll.2974-3681, to follow Owen's translation, *14*) has only 25.7% direct speech and, even if it is taken with the first part (ll.2525-2844, whose percentage at 43.9 approximates well to the immediately preceding context), the episode as a whole contains only 31.4% direct speech. But this merely reflects the needs of the narrative at this point: much of the episode is the story of fighting, and there is little room for discussion or argument. The most nearly comparable section of Roland's battle, the 503 lines up to the Second Horn Scene (ll.1187-1690) produces a percentage of only 19.7 direct speech.

The point here is that the whole manner of the narrative changes radically once the moral arguments on which so much stress was laid in Chapter 2 above are over. The percentage up to the start of the fighting at line 1187 is 58.3, and indeed for the first 660 lines, up to the departure of Ganelon from Marsile's court, it is as high as 64.5. These statistics are a measure of the importance placed by the author on the ethical problems which he wants to have debated, and this use of space must be set against the view that moral issues, and the characterisation which inevitably comes out of the debate, are of little importance in comparison with the tragic action (see especially Hunt, *56, 86* ; cf. van Emden, *162*).

It is a corollary of this statistical analysis that the first part of the poem has a radically different narrative technique from the accounts of fighting, though of course a further ethical discussion, with profound implications for the moral conception of the characters involved, is inserted into the battle of Roncevaux: the Second Horn Scene. We have looked at the way in which this scene is structured, and the light this structure itself throws on the poet's intentions (Chapter 2, pp.63-64). But this is only one example of the techniques involved (see van Emden, *162*). There is no space here to analyse them in detail; the essential point for our present purposes is the way in which the poet puts contrasting moral and tactical opinions before us without significant intervention on his part, except in the way he chooses to structure the discussion (cf. the silence of Ganelon, Chapter 2, p.29), allowing us to form our own opinions, and this over a very significant proportion of his text. The style becomes much more narrative once the fighting starts.

There is, by contrast, one aspect of the author's manner which does involve his presence in the text and his complicity with the audience. I refer to the common apostrophes directed implicitly to the latter and commenting on events, predicting or bewailing the coming disaster, e.g. ll.9, 95 (these linked by echo), 179, 511, 608, 716 (see Hemming note), 812-13, 858-59, 1401-03, 1436-37, 1690, 1806 (linked with 1840-41), 1849-50, 1885, 1886-88, 1912, 1913, 2009 (linked thematically with Oliver's line, 1977), 2082, 2095-98, 2245 (thematically linked with Roland's line, 2258), 2524, 3025, 3164, 3381-82, 3393-95, 3403-04, 3473-74, 3480, 3577-78 (linked with 3587-88, 3914), 3742-43, 3872 (linked with Charlemagne's line 3891, Tierri's line 3898), 3959 and 3974 (linked thematically), 4002.

This contact between author (or singer) and audience is increased by the fact that the interjection *as* or *ais*, 'behold' is always followed by a personal pronoun as indirect object. Sometimes this may be the third person, *li* (ll.2452, 3495, 3708, 3818), in which case the phrase remains embedded in the narrative. But more frequently the pronoun is *vos, vus*: ll.263, 413, 889, 1187, 1889, 1989, 2009, 3403, which allies singer and hearer, reader and poet in one community. Similar effects are produced by the hemistich *la veïs(s)ez* (ll.349, 1655, 3388) and, in the very first line, by the possessive adjective *nostre*, applied to the emperor, and implying a common patriotic French or Christian identity for audience and performer. The same word, as adjective or pronoun, sometimes plural as *(li, les) noz*, recurs in the author's own voice at ll.1190, 1444, 2504, 2872, 3085; it is much commoner in the speech of Christian characters, which gives something of the same effect at one remove; when given to Saracens, e.g. line 1951, it evokes for the hearers a hostile community, in opposition to their own.

Yet such methods are used with discretion. The poet might have made frequent use of the four-syllable formula *nostre emperere* in place of the common *li emperere(s)* in the first hemistich, but (with the proviso that scribes may have intervened) he seems to choose not to do so. His many apostrophes are his closest contact with the audience, yet he avoids the most direct one: *'Oiez, (seignor)!'* and other personal forms of address which later writers of romance, such as Marie de France and Béroul, not to speak of epic authors, will use frequently. *Sauf erreur*, the verb *oïr* is used with reference to the hearers only at ll.2023, 3248. The direct imperative to the audience, so common in later *chansons de geste* in particular, is almost absent here.

A last feature of narrative technique, called 'interlace' in analysis of romances, and 'cross-cutting' in cinematographic terms (which I prefer for the more dramatic epic) requires mention. It is not uncommon in *chansons de geste* of all periods to transfer attention from one character or place to another, though epic *time* usually remains linear. Most poets announce such departures rather crudely: 'Mes or lerons ci atant d'Olivier,/qant leus sera bien savrai reperier' (*Girart de Vienne*, 20, ll.2978-79) is typical. The transitions in *Roland* are subtler: the transfer to and from Marsile's court for Ganelon's message is done simply by saying that Ganelon departs: ll.365, 660; at line 661 we precede him back to Charles, who is waiting for news from him (line 665), but Ganelon arrives at the end of the same laisse. In cinematographic terms, again, one might speak of 'lap-dissolve'.

The next important change of scene, from Roland's nomination to the rearguard to the Saracen court for the boasts of the pagan peers, comes in laisse LXVIII. The fear of Charles for his nephew leads to an evocation of Ganelon's treason (line 844), then the gifts he has had from Marsile (ll.845-47), and so to the latter's summoning of his men and the scene of the boasts. When it is over, the transition back, now to the rearguard rather than Charles, is equally smooth: the last boast culminates in a general gathering of the pagans and their arming (ll.990-93), which is taken up at the start of the next laisse (LXXIX). The description of the Saracen host is vivid and occupies half the laisse; at line 1004 their bugles are blown, and line 1005, the median line of the laisse, transfers the great noise from the pagans (first hemistich) to the French (second hemistich).

The transfers from Roland, when he does blow the horn, to Charles and the army are achieved simply with the 'voice' of the olifant (ll.1755-57, 1765-67, 1787-88; 2103-05), though at the end of the first three of the laisses involved (CXXXIII-CXXXV) the return to the field of battle has to be by 'cross-cutting', since Roland cannot yet be allowed to hear the army's response. Laisses CXXXIII and CXXXIV build up to Ganelon's scornful lie, so that the transfer back to Roncevaux is inevitable, given the inaction of the king, and underlines the predicament Roland is in. Then, after Naimon's turning the table on the traitor (CXXXV), we stay with the army's frenzied preparations for the return till CXXXIX, which transits back to the battlefield via the regret of the warriors that they are not with Roland (ll.1845-47) and the personal intervention of the author describing Roland's weak state and the sixty survivors (ll.1848-50). Thus the hopelessness of the hero's situation prepares, in a smooth transition, the bleak look around the hillsides with which he opens the crucial laisse CXL. Later, at CLVI, of course, the transfer back can at last be through the sound of the army's trumpets, and it reaches both Saracens and Christians (ll.2113-51) to precipitate the final phase of the battle.

These analyses may serve to show the mastery with which this poet manages his transitions from one scene to another. We must now examine the equal proficiency with which he handles the laisse.

The structure of the laisse in the *Roland* has become, rightly or wrongly, a benchmark for other epics. The average length, if we use Whitehead's stanza-division, and treat his CXXVa as a separate laisse, is 13.38 lines, and the extreme limits are 5 (XXVI, LX) and 34 (CCXXXI). The starting point for a study of strophic structure in the *chanson de geste* is still the excellent chapter on the subject in Rychner (*138*, pp.68-125, though I do not endorse the implied conclusions for oral composition). Most of the laisses in our poem may be likened to a good paragraph in an expository essay in that they deal with one motif or narrative episode, and one only. A *vers d'intonation*, usually a complete sentence and very often containing the name of a character, his title or a collective noun like *paien*, sets a topic (sometimes a summing-up of what has preceded). The rest of the laisse develops this, while a *vers de conclusion* rounds it off (though often leading on also to the next laisse) in what is frequently a memorable, lapidary way (p.123 below). Examples of this structure, which probably corresponds to the musical pattern (Hemming, *1*, x-xi, Suard, *148*, pp.12-13), are laisses III, IV, VIII, XII, XVI, XXX, LVI-LVII, LXIX, LXXXIX, XCI, XCIII, CVI, CIX, CXIII, CXV, etc.; in truth, these are chosen almost at random, and most laisses have a basic unity of content which is most striking, and which contrasts strongly with poems only thirty or forty years later, like the *Couronnement Louis*. This is not necessarily a value-judgement, rather a measure of difference in technique and purpose, cf. Heinemann (*80*, pp.23-26, 167-77).

This feature of relatively short laisses allows the optimum development of *laisses similaires* and *laisses parallèles*, since of course it becomes progressively more difficult, aesthetically as well as thematically, to repeat with minimum variation the content of laisses as they lengthen (commonly reaching hundreds of lines in thirteenth-century epics). I shall return to the general subject of '*similaire* technique' later, but summarise Rychner's definitions (*138*, pp.83-107) here. In *laisses similaires*, the same narrative material is repeated on different assonances (e.g. LXXXIII-LXXXV, CLXXIV-CLXXVI); in *laisses parallèles* different narrative material, such as the successive deaths of several heroes, is treated in similar terms on separate assonances (e.g. XLVIII-XLIX, XCVII-CI, CLXII-CLXIII, CCXXIV-CCXXVI) – the number of laisses is often, but not necessarily, three in both types.

But the *laisse similaire/parallèle* is only one aspect of the patterns of repetition which characterise the Old French epic, which give it an incantatory quality (Hemming, *1*, p.xxvi) and to which the term 'echo' is increasingly being applied (for the fullest development of the aesthetic of echo, see Heinemann, *80*, Troisième Partie). This feature is admirably characterised, in both its probable origins and its artistic effect, by Suard (*148*, pp.4-5):

> [. . .] le caractère formulaire de l'écriture épique, loin de signaler une défaillance, invite le lecteur à rechercher, au-delà de procédés mnémotechniques liés au caractère oral du genre en ses débuts, un réseau complexe d'échos, fait de reprises et de variations, sur lequel se fonde la puissance émotionnelle du texte.

It is important to understand the emotional effect of most forms of repetition, from the roll of drums which once drove armies into battle, overcoming the inhibitions of the cannon-fodder advancing towards the sound of gunfire, to the patterns of repetition, including rhythm and rhyme as well as refrain, which characterise many forms of poetry and are at their most concentrated in lyric poetry.

The early *chansons de geste* have indeed much in common with the latter.

The emotional force of rhythm and repetitive patterns may have something to do with the satisfaction of anticipation, with the predictable return of the expected word or sound (cf. Heinemann, *78*, p.19). There is certainly no doubting the affective nature of such devices as alliteration, assonance and rhyme, and of rhetorical figures involving repetition, notably *anaphora*. This important figure, defined as 'the repetition of the same word or words at the beginning of successive clauses' (Curtius, *52*, p.44), is particularly successful in moving the hearer, in swaying opinions, and it is significant that it occurs commonly, and instinctively, in speeches by modern politicians who have never heard the term. There are a few formal examples in the *Roland*, at e.g. ll.1031-33, 1399-403, and it is probably no accident that there is a cluster around the deaths of Turpin and Roland at ll.2210-13, 2377-80 and 2402-05. (Further examples arise almost automatically, and therefore less affectively, from the setting up of *escheles* in the Baligant episode, e.g. ll.3224-30, 3240-46.)

Perhaps anaphora, which can sometimes occur in alternating lines in formal examples, gives us a hint as to why echo, even at a distance, is so effective in moving the hearer or reader. Certainly, the poem is full of repetition, both close and at a distance, and it may be that the very return of motifs, words or formulae already used, though not regularly as in formal anaphora, and even involving some variation in form, nevertheless retains something of that figure's incantatory power to move us.

Some such echoes may be simply affective, adding intensity to the account of an important episode. A fine example occurs between lines 1401 and 1422. Here there is a complex reprise of the last two lines of CIX and the first of CX, which themselves transfer the scene from the rearguard (ll.1401-02) to the main army (ll.1403, 1404). After this transfer (by 'cross-cutting'), the rest of CX uses the impossibility of aid (line 1405, connecting army and rearguard) to justify foretelling the punishment of Ganelon in France, before the start of CXI returns to the rearguard's struggle. Then line 1420 echoes line 1401, both evoking the losses of the French, while the first hemistich of line 1402, *Ne reverrunt*, is picked up textually by the first of line 1421, whose second hemistich modulates from *lor meres ne lor femmes* (in France, line 1402) to *lor pers ne lor parenz*, who may be either in the main army or at home. Finally, line 1422 combines echoes from lines 1403 (second hemistich) and 1404 (first hemistich), before line 1423 goes back, beyond the passes evoked in *ki as porz les atent/atendent*, to France itself (cf. line 1403), for the cosmic signs of Roland's death. This celebrated passage is thus introduced in an atmosphere already heightened emotionally by the heavy use of interlacing echo.

It is no accident, surely, that the same device is used at moments when the olifant itself rouses the echoes of the high hills (ll.1753-1846, 2099-150). The echoes, here too, occur within a complex and varying context: one might speak of elements of *similaire* material which are not all organised into formal *laisses similaires* or *laisses parallèles*. There is no space to analyse each scene in the detailed way just applied to ll.1401-22, but I offer here the references of linked lines in the two passages in which the olifant is sounded. (The symbol = indicates a link; 'a' and 'b' indicate first and second hemistichs respectively.)

(1) 1753-54 = 1761-64 = 1785-87; 1755a (which of course picks up this evocative hemistich from 814-15, where the full motif first appears, cf.2271) = 1830-31; 1755b-1756 = 1765 = 1789b; 1757 = 1766-67 = 1788; 1758 = 1768-69 = 1789; 1759-60 = 1770-84 = (with change of speaker and message) 1790-95.

Thus far, with the exception of the echo at ll.1830-31, we have rather loosely constructed *laisses similaires* (CXXXIII-CXXXV) in which the last motif, Ganelon's reply, is vastly developed in the second stanza, and replaced by, and contrasted with, Naimon's intervention in the third. This conforms to the type of repetition called *reprise bifurquée* by Rychner (*138*, pp.80-86), and we will return to it. For the moment, given that one motif in the set, 1755a, is not echoed until ll.1830-31, we will continue the analysis of the whole first passage. The repetitions now become much less exact and organised, and there is no echo for the long description of Ganelon's treatment (ll.1816-29).

1797b = 1793a; 1798-800 = 1808-11; 1801-02 = 1812-13 = 1834-35 = 1842-44; 1814 = 1836; 1803-05 = ?1815 = 1837-39 = 1845-46 (at which point the reference to Roland is used for a transition back to the battlefield); 1806 = 1840-41 (cf. 1405 in the earlier scene, and 1913).

The second passage in which the olifant is sounded (ll.2099-150) is the one which leads to the flight of the remaining Saracens, and it has some echo at a distance from the passage just analysed, as well as complex internal patterns of repetition.

(2) 2102 = 1764 = 1786; 2104 = 1753-54 = 1761-62 = 1787; 2105-08 = 1758 = 1768-69 = 1789; 2110 = ?1796; 2111-12 = 1832-33; the last two lines of CLVI move away from this system of echo from the first horn-blowing scene to introduce the reaction of the Saracens which, with that of Roland and Turpin, will occupy the rest of the present passage. There is again a complex system of echo:

2115 = 2133 = 2145 = 2149 (the first and last being spoken by Saracens, the second and third by the two Christians); 2116 = 2132 = 2150 (here the Christians have only line 2132, and the motif of the sound of the horn is omitted in CLIX). Another source of echo in this passage is the first hemistich of each of the five laisses involved, each referring either to Roland or the pagans, but this is part of the manner of the poet: we have already seen that there is a very general tendency throughout the poem (including the Baligant episode) for the name or title of a character, or a group like *paien*, to appear in the first line of a laisse, particularly in the first hemistich.

A pattern like those examined in these two examples may be found also at ll.824-841, where line 824, the last but one line of LXVI, is picked up by the first line of LXVII, while line 825 is echoed by the first line of LXVIII. For somewhat similar patterns from the Baligant episode, see 3004 = 3025, 3041 = 3048, 3577 = 3587, 3623 = 3625 = 3634 = 3648.

Echo between the first lines of laisses is common, as is that between *vers de conclusion*: e.g (first lines) 62 = 78; 244-45 = 252-

53 = 274-76; 377 = 392; 3658 = (with antithetical inversion) 3675; 3975 = 3988; they need not necessarily come in adjacent laisses, e.g. 441 = 485; 512 = 563 = 580; 931 = 940 = 975; 1017 = 1028 etc.; (last lines) 9 = 95; 724 = 736; 908 = 974; 915 = 929-30 = 939; 3578 = 3914 (crossing the boundary of the Baligant episode); 3959 = 3974. Again,. it is common for a *vers d'intonation* to pick up a *vers de conclusion*, forming a natural transition as well as providing echo: 138 = 139; at 441-42, the first two lines of XXXIV pick up 438-39 from near the end of XXXIII; 873 = 874; 993 = 994, etc. It would be easy to multiply such examples; I limit myself here to roughly the first quarter, and the end, of the poem, and make no use of *laisses similaires* at this point.

Echo may be used, sometimes at considerable distance, to stress elements of importance to the poet. There are considerable similarities between Oliver's words at ll.1099-1105, 1170-74 and 1715-36; in particular, the use of the verb *deignier* in relation to Roland's refusal to sound the horn (ll.1101, 1171, 1716) makes an important point about Oliver's view of Roland's pride, and there are also, in the speeches of both men in the Second Horn Scene, precise echoes of the First, though Roland at ll.1702-04 speaks Oliver's ll.1071-72 while Oliver's ll.1701, 1705-07 parallel Roland's ll.1091, 1063, 1076. Further, Oliver repeats his own earlier arguments (ll.1102, 1174) with his ll.1717-18.

Other examples of repetition for emphasis (ignoring for the moment such *laisses similaires* as the First Horn Scene) might include the incantatory echo of the first hemistich *En Rencesvals* in the boasts of the Saracen peers at ll.901, 912, 923, 934, 944, 963, 985 (it appears in the second hemistich at line 892). We are not dealing with formal *laisses similaires* or *parallèles* here, but the stanzas devoted to the peers contain other *similaire* material, such as the idea of swords red with blood, and the peers will reappear and fight in precisely the same order at the start of the battle (XCIII-CIV). The fateful step-relationship, and with it the crucial moment when Roland nominates Ganelon, are emphasised by the formal parallelism of the latter's line 743 with the former's much earlier line 277. Roland's feudal credo of ll.1010-14 is reinforced by echo at ll.1117-21, on the other side of the First Horn Scene. The gravity of treason is underlined by two successive and memorably similar *vers de conclusion* at ll.3959, 3974.

Sometimes, echo can be used to stress contrast. When Ganelon echoes Roland's *Ja mar crerez Marsilie* (line 196) with *Ja mar crerez bricun* (line 220), the poet is showing the stepfather's opposition to, and contempt for, the stepson. The parallelism of *Je vos plevis* at ll.1069, 1072 emphasises the contrasting views of Roland and Oliver; and there is another sort of difference brought out when ll.1071-72 are echoed at ll.1703-04: the inversion by which Roland now espouses Oliver's earlier plea. At ll.751-52 and 761-62, parallel *vers d'intonation* introduce divergent second lines, followed by contrasting speeches.

We are dealing here with a good example of Rychner's *reprise bifurquée* (see Rychner, *138*, pp.80-86 and above, p.109). We saw earlier that the rather loose *laisses similaires* CXXXIII-CXXXV also conform to this pattern: in the first two, the sounding of the olifant and Charlemagne's reaction lead to the cynical efforts of Ganelon to prevent or delay the return of the army; the third time, the same motifs lead to a contrast: Naimon, not Ganelon, replies, and he urges speedy aid for Roland, while pointing the finger of accusation at the traitor. The contrast is the sharper for the similarity of the first parts of each laisse. Rychner (p.80) applies the analysis to laisses CCLXXII-CCLXXIII (Whitehead numbers), but these seem to conform less well to the type, which is not plentiful in *Roland*, at least at the level of the full laisse. One might argue that the two pairs of dreams (LVI-LVII and CLXXXV-CLXXXVI) represent an inversion of the *reprise bifurquée*: the first dream in each case describes a different battle, and in rather different terms, while the second dreams, rather similar to each other, both prophesy the punishment of Ganelon.

The idea of *reprise bifurquée* may perhaps be extended to a feature of the poet's manner which has always struck me: he occasionally (and especially in the 'exposition') uses similar contexts to draw something significant to the hearers' attention by repeating it with increasing precision. When Ganelon starts to rage at Roland in the nomination scene he makes a vague threat of vengeance at ll.289-91 which is little more than mouthing in anger. By the next laisse, he has linked his threat with the mission to Marsile (ll.299-301), and this is repeated in the menacing last line of XXV. He is shown to be ready for Blancandrin's advances. When these come in XXVIII, a non-committal answer about Charles turns in the next two laisses to precise descriptions of Roland as the chief 'hawk' of the Frankish army. The *laisses similaires* XL-XLII furnish a third example of this method: to very similar questions about Charlemagne, Ganelon first praises the emperor, while stressing that *he* is not warlike (ll.529-36); in the next two laisses, Marsile is told first that Charles's 'nephew' is the obstacle (ll.544-49) and then he is given the fateful name (ll.557-62), the assonance bringing it to the end of the line, in place of *nies* (line 544). Then, in the sequel to the series, the two terms twice come together: *sis nies, li quens Rollant* (ll.575, 585). Marsile by this time is persuaded (line 581). A similar technique is used for Ganelon's two aggressive versions of Charlemagne's message (XXXIII, XXXVI) by which, at the risk of his life, he seeks to focus the fear and anger of Marsile on Roland. The latter's name emerges only in the second version (line 473), accompanied by a threatening epithet (line 474) and associated with specific new details of humiliation (ll.479-81, cf. line 437) to add to the threat of death 'by judgement' which appears in both (ll.435-37, 482). One might add the way in which the hostages are sometimes omitted from the various repetitions of the Saracen offer at the start, in order to be brought back (because they are the crucial element for credibility) by dramatic technique, or the way Ganelon's plan is revealed with increasing detail in XLIII-XLV. In all these cases, the added precision comes out of much *similaire* material, even when it is not a matter of formal *laisses similaires*.

In its most developed examples, the *laisse similaire* is a formalised extension of such methods, though it is also a lyrical element, whose echoes, coming thick and fast in a short passage, heighten the emotion in a special way. Rychner (*138*, pp.93-107) deals magisterially with the different types of *laisses similaires* and *parallèles*, and the way in which the method is adapted in poems with longer laisses. He very accurately describes the *Roland* author's contribution to the technique (p.93):

> C'est incontestablement l'auteur du *Roland* qui a tiré le meilleur parti de la vertu lyrique des ensembles de laisses similaires; ses groupes de trois laisses similaires arrêtent le récit aux moments les plus dramatiques, les plus décisifs, formant comme des barrages, de hautes haltes lyriques, avant que de nouveau la narration reprenne son cours.

The image of a dam, a horizontal obstacle in the vertical path of the narrative, after which the latter rushes on with renewed vigour, is a very appropriate one. There are a number of examples of *laisses similaires* in our poem, more or less formally ordered (e.g. XL-XLII, LXXXIII-LXXXV, CXXXIII-CXXXV, CLXXIV-CLXXVI, CCVII-CCVIII, CCIX-CCX). I intend to analyse two examples, one 'static', the other 'dynamic' (a further distinction I would wish to establish, alongside Rychner's own between *laisses similaires* and *laisses parallèles*, which was summarised above, p.107).

Laisses LXXXIII-LXXXV (for present purposes I-III) make up the First Horn Scene, a perfect example of a 'static' series of *laisses similaires*, in which a given number of motifs recurs, in this case over three laisses, with no omission or addition to their number, though with some 'incremental repetition', as ballad specialists would say. The purpose seems to be not only the decorative lyrical heightening of the emotions which has been mentioned, but also to stress the tactical and moral attitudes represented by Roland and Oliver, since these underlie the moral conception of the subject (see Chapter 2).

If one counts the lines in each of the three laisses, these number respectively 10, 11 and 12 lines. In fact, the first two lines of laisse I refer back to the theme of the previous laisses, and are merely the link between the lyrical passage and its context. The *similaire* material is therefore contained in 8, 10 and 12 lines; this is the measure of the incremental repetition which takes place in some, but not all, the motifs which are now to be identified.

(1) *Cumpaign Rollant, kar sunez vostre corn*: ll.1051, 1059, 1070 (no increment). The request to sound the horn is introduced in each laisse by the same first-hemistich formula, which by its content implies dramatic opposition. That the horn is made of ivory (*olifant* may almost be a proper noun like *Durendal*) is, caracteristically, reserved to the second laisse, and sent to the assonance for extra stress in the third.

(2) *Si l'orrat Carles...*: ll.1052, 1060-61, 1071-72 (increments 1:2:2). This recurring first-hemistich formula is completed by the promise that the Franks will return, expanded in laisses II and III and increasing in urgency to the intense *je vos plevis* of line 1072 (to be taken up, as we have seen, by Roland in the Second Horn Scene, ll.1703-04).

(3) *Respunt Rollant...*: ll.1053, 1062, 1073 (no increment). This phrase recurs in each laisse, strikingly sent to the assonance in III, and is accompanied by a refusal in categorical terms: *Jo fereie que fols, Ne placet (Damne)deu*. In accordance with this self-evidently dramatic technique, Roland now gives his reasons for this refusal.

(4) The motif of reputation: ll.1054, 1063-64, 1074-76 (increment 1:2:3). It is no doubt significant that this central plank in Roland's motivation receives such dramatic incremental repetition, leading to the contemptuous *Ne pur paien que ja seie cornant!*

(5) The expectation of striking great blows: ll.1055-56, 1065-67, 1077-79 (increment 2:3:3). The name of Durendal recurs each time, as does the promise of staining it with blood; and the expression becomes increasingly personal: *jo serai . . . jo ferrai*.

(6) A promise of total victory: ll.1057-58, 1068-69, 1080-81 (2:2:2, no increment, but two lines' worth of emphasis each time).

The basis of the great controversy between the two friends is thus clearly established in dramatic terms which allow the audience to judge, but also with a lyrical intensity which raises the emotional temperature of the narrative. There is total stasis, apart from the increments, in the number of motifs, for this, as we saw in Chapter 2 (pp.48-49), is a *dialogue de sourds*. It should be noted, however, that the series is not separated from the following narrative by an obvious change of course or tone: the argument continues on the same issues for some time, and the ends of the next five laisses (LXXXVI-XC) all continue the motif of striking blows, echoing motif (5).

Laisses CLXXIV-CLXXVI (I-III for purposes of analysis), which recount the death of Roland, are what I would call a 'dynamic' series of *laisses similaires*. They come as the third of three groups of three laisses each which lead from the death of Turpin to that of Roland (CLXVIII-CLXXVI; see Chapter 2, pp.71-74). In 'dynamic' *laisses similaires*, some motifs fade as others are added, so that there is a progression which may be likened to waves on a beach when the tide is coming in. The motifs in these laisses are as follows (for comment on the significance of each, see the discussion in Chapter 2).

(1) Realisation that death is close: ll.2355-56, 2366, so in I and II only, and fading out.

(2) The place. This refers back to, and explains, the first group of three laisses (I assume that the movements described at ll.2298, 2357 are intended to be within the site chosen at ll.2265-70). Lines 2357-63, 2367, 2375-6, occupying most of I, where the olifant and Durendal are recalled, and the significance of the choice of place is explained; fading abruptly to one and two lines in II and III, where nevertheless *De(En)vers Espaigne* stresses the symbolism of that choice.

(3) *Mea culpa*: ll.2364, 2369-72, 2377-88, one line in I, greatly expanded in II (5 lines) and enormously so in III (12 lines), where the motif incorporates the hero's dying memories generally and a short liturgical prayer (*credo épique*).

(4) The offer of the glove: ll.2365, 2373, 2389. No increment, but the motif is the last in I, the next to last in II as a new motif appears:

(5) The presence of angels: ll.2374, 2390. In II and III only; in III, Gabriel himself takes the glove, while the other angels are named at ll.2394-95 as part of:

(6) The death: ll.2391-96, only in III, glorified by the names of the three angels, carrying the emotive overtones detailed in Chapter 2 (p.74).

These overtones, along with the protective ones associated with *Veire Patene (imago paterna)*, the faith that God has never failed His people (*ki unkes ne mentis*, with recollection of Lazarus and Daniel), the lyrical repetition of *cleimet sa culpe/Deus, meie culpe*, the proffered glove with its multiple symbolism, all these, with the 'overlapping wave' effect, make these 'dynamic' laisses into a lyrically heightened moment different from the 'static' series analysed above, but emotionally at least equally powerful. (For an excellent analysis, to which mine is intended to be complementary, see Vinaver, *168*, pp.62-68.)

This analysis of the *laisse similaire* technique is only one aspect of the use of language affectively throughout. Individual words or images often carry overtones which heighten the emotional power of the text. We saw, in Chapter 2, a number of marked uses of the adjective *saive*, which, with its cognates *sage, save(i)r*, means 'wise', 'wisdom' but which, as Misrahi and Henderson (*112*, pp.366-67; *113*, pp.229-30) show, sometimes 'keeps bad company': it is frequently used by or about Saracens or Ganelon, and therefore often carries a menacing charge of wisdom used for an evil purpose (see ll.20, 24, 74, 279, 369, 426, 569, 648, 3174, 3279, 3509, 3774; I do not accept Misrahi and Henderson's illogical conclusion that these words are therefore pejorative wherever else they are used).

Formulaic style, as in Homer, produces affective overtones intensified by the inherent repetition. France is ever *dulce*, as we have noted, contrasting with *clere Espaigne la bele*, line 59; it is also called *tere major*, 'the great land', ll.600, 952, 1532, 1667, 1784, or 'land of the ancestors' (line 818; for the applicability of both meanings, see Walker, *169*); at line 819, the very words *la tere*, coupled with *lor seignur*, carry an emotional charge in keeping with the tears shed at the sight of it. Both these repeated concepts become leitmotivs whose affective overtones receive lyrical expression in Roland's enthusiasm about a vassal's duty towards his lord (ll.1010-16, 1117-23) and his concern for France's honour (ll.1064, 1210, 1861, 1927, etc.). The same applies to *reis* (e.g. ll.1121, 2133) and *emperere*, a word which, with the grandiose adjectives *nostre* and *magnes*, fills the second hemistich of the first line (cf. ll.703, 841, 1195). The emperor's very name is of course heavy with the great Charlemagne myth (see Folz, *69*; Bender, *33*, pp.9-26). Other words which have valorising, if not always precise, connotations are *proz, ber/baron/barnage/barnét* (the abstract nouns meaning either 'company of barons' or 'knighthood, courage', the latter meanings giving positive overtones to the former), *cortois*, etc. *Cataigne*, basically a military title, 'commander', also implies, emotionally, the valour associated with such a man (ll.1846, 2320, 3709). Ganelon, by contrast, is already from the start, the man *ki la traïsun fist* (line 178), so that all his actions and words take on a special menace, and episodes such as the kiss from Marsile (line 601), and the Saracen presents which follow, take on Judas overtones, as, probably, does line 178 (cf. Luke 6. 16, Matthew 10. 4). Other words in that semantic field are *traïr, traïtre/traïtur, fel(s)/felon*, while *culvert, caitif*, etc. carry more general pejorative meanings, again vague enough to have resonance.

Proper nouns are used to similar effect: all but one (line 2209) of the place-names involving the word *Val* are in Saracen country, implying shadowy places of menace (cf. the Valley of the Shadow of Death in Psalm 23); almost all the anthroponyms beginning *Mar-*, including Marsilie, and all those beginning *Mal-* are also applied to pagans, with striking results such as *Malbien*, line 67, with its shocking oxymoron, or *Malcuid* and *Malquiant*, both line 1594, where the prefix is combined with forms of the verb *cuidier*, 'to think, to believe' (often erroneously), carrying implications of false belief. Other eloquent pagan names include *Abisme*, line 1470, *Chernuble de Munigre*, line 975, *Margariz*, ll.955, 1310-11, implying apostasy (*1*, p.176). On the other hand, some Saracen names are seductively musical: *Cazmarines*, line 956, *Balide*, line

3230, *Baldise*, line 3255, *Valfunde*, line 23. Laisse V shows a moderate and euphonic exoticism rather than the grotesque pagan names of later epics, although, as Hemming observes (*1*, n.63), none of the names is Arabic in origin; and the name of *Blancandrins*, line 23, etc., is also euphonic, and evokes the wise counsellor's white hair. It is clear that any reference to *Francs*, *Franceis*, *France*, *la Geste Francor* is bathed in patriotic fervour, as is shown particularly by the expression *Francs/Franceis de France* at ll.804, 808; no doubt the proper nouns carry some of the connotations of the adjective *franc*, 'free, noble'.

There is a good deal of effective symbolism, some of which is consistent over long stretches of the narrative, like the image of 'Charlemagne's right arm' for Roland, which is exploited also in the symmetrical loss of Marsile's right hand. I analysed this in Chapter 2 (pp.39, 42, 55, 67), where I argued also (p.66) that the 'bear' symbol characterises Ganelon throughout, though we have to suppose that the Digby manuscript for once has an error when it writes *ver(s)* 'boar' for *ur(s)* in laisse LVII. Similarly, we have seen already that Ganelon at times evokes overtones of Judas, though it is dangerous to take this idea too far (e.g. Brault, *7*, p.155, on Marsile's kiss for Ganelon: Judas did not kiss the High Priest, as it were, but Jesus!). The corollary of seeing Ganelon simply as Judas would be to see Roland as symbolising Christ; but this would be more convincing if Roland died at the hands of the Saracens, as in the *Pseudo-Turpin*, rather than by his own efforts to recall Charlemagne. That there are overtones of the Passion and indeed the Parousia in the signs which foretell Roland's death (ll.1423-37, see Chapter 2, pp.57-58) is true, but it is also true that such cosmic signs are part of the epic and tragic paradigm of the death of the hero.

The poet is himself aware of the classical symbolism of olive-branches (ambassadors bear them in four passages of the *Aeneid*, cf. *Roman d'Eneas*, ca. 1160, *17*, ll.4687-88, etc.; see *3*, n.72, 80), and he draws the audience's attention to it (ll.72-73). Brault (*7*, pp.141-43) is certainly right to point to Ganelon's story about Roland's giving Charlemagne a red apple representing the crowns of all

kings (ll.383-88) as symbolising not only the forbidden fruit of
Genesis but also the temptation of Christ by Satan (cf. Chapter 2,
pp.33-34). On the symbolism of the animals in the dreams, see
especially Steinmeyer, *146*, p.44ff., Braet, *40*, pp.147-50, van
Emden, *158*. Unfortunately, as with number symbolism, animal
symbolism is subject to many contradictory interpretations.
Symbolism seems to me to be incidental and much less common in
Roland than it does to some critics. It will be apparent that I cannot
in general follow Brault's ubiquitous application of the methods of
mediaeval biblical exegesis, including symbolism and allegory, on
the grounds that this constitutes a 'medieval reading' (*7*, pp.30-32),
to anything in the poem which may thus be made to support his
overall interpretation, if only because the results so frequently
contradict utterly the *sensus* or surface meaning, and because the
parallels proposed are often extremely arbitrary, far-fetched and
incapable of verification or disproof: see, e.g. pp.132, 178, 184, 198,
249-50, etc.

Signs of the learned literary tradition propagated by the
schools are rarer than in, say, most later romances, much of the
rhetoric being the natural result of composition for oral performance
(cf. Suard's comments on formulaic style and its conscious
application to literary ends, p.107 above, and the discussion
following). Nevertheless, there is substantial evidence for the formal
education of the author. The *locus amoenus* ('agreeable place')
topos, for example, is at least adumbrated in the shady places (cf.
verger, ll.11, 159) in which we first meet both Marsile and Charles
(laisses II, VIII, XI) and the place in which Roland chooses to die
(ll.2357-58); a number of the elements of the complete topos are not
used (see Curtius, *52*, pp.185-90, 192-202; Brault, *7*, p.67) but the
passages concerned visibly exploit the tradition. A further topos is
ubi sunt (*Ubi sunt qui ante nos in hoc mondo fuere?* 'Where are
those who were in the world before us?', Siciliano, *144*, pp.256-61),
expressed partly in fine anaphoric form in Charlemagne's *planctus*
at ll.2402-10.

We have already discussed the figure of *anaphora* above, and
seen that there are few formal examples in the text (see however

ll.2210-13, 2377-80), but that echoes throughout the text have much the same rhetorical effect. In the context of rhetoric, ll.63-68 may be seen as an example of the figure *accumulatio*, 'enumeration' (cf. Hemming, *1*, n.63ff.); see too ll.30-33, 183-86, 398-99, 711-13, 820-21, 845-50, 1084-85, 1663-64, 1968-69, 1979, 2074-75, 2420-21, 2921-24, 3410-11, etc., as well as 793-98, 1031-33, 2186-89, 2322-32, 3306-08, which also contain a measure of somewhat irregular anaphora; these examples, like ll.814-15, 980-82, 1041-43, 1010-12, 1117-19, 1399-1400, etc., show complex patterns in which there is accumulation not only of one part of speech but of two or more, in rough alternation. Such patterns involve echo in very close order, and may therefore be seen not only as part of the learned rhetorical tradition, but also (or alternatively) as belonging to the general tendency to echo inherent in formulaic composition. There is, too, a very fine case of *conduplicatio* (word-repetition for emphasis) if line 2183 is corrected 'Cist camp est vostre, mercit Deu, [vostre] e mien' as indicated by Samaran's ultra-violet light reading; cf. ll.249, 460-61, 2004, 2436-38.

There are occasional examples of other 'flowers of rhetoric': ll.1492-95 are all on a chiastic pattern of adjective: noun: noun: adjective, and *chiasmus* is a favourite figure of rhetorically-trained writers, as well as involving patterns of echo; see e.g. ll.229, 284, 814, 1755, 2004, 2943, 3345, 3658-59. But for the uneven division of the decasyllabic line by the caesura, one might often (e.g. ll.8, 54, 215, 229, 284, 297, 569, 1100, 1199-1200, 2029, 2112, 2943, 3055, 3633, 3658-59, 3675, etc.) speak of *isocolon*: the balancing of contiguous clauses of equal length and, usually, parallel structure. At the level of successive lines, this figure may be said to occur e.g. at ll.2322-25, 2385-86, 2706-07, as well as many of the laisses, e.g CCXXXVII, in which *escheles* are set up; though here again there is overlap between rhetorical figure and echo effect born of formulaic composition. The figure *antithesis* (sometimes in conjunction with chiasmus and isocolon) is not uncommon (e.g. ll.229, 297, 569, 724, 736, 737, 814, 1011, 1015, 1100, 1118, 1162-63, 2030, 2895, 3554, 3658, 3675). *Litotes* (understatement) is found at e.g. ll.306, 323, 1481, 1484, 1528, 1901, etc. *Interrogatio* (rhetorical question) figures prominently in the *planctus* referred to above, and at e.g. ll.286, 603, 764-65, 1806, 2812, 2961, 3339, 3611, 3956, etc.; *exclamatio* is inevitably common too, e.g. ll.350, 467, 716, 1073-75, 1604, 1632, 1669-70, 1898, 1938, 2898-900, 3340, 3386-88, etc. The author uses brief *similes* (e.g. ll.890, 977-78, 1111, 1474-76, 1535, 1572, 1616, 1874-75, 3318-19, 3503, 3520-21, 3527). These mainly describe people or horses; the series at ll.1535-1616 (plus line 1598, which is not strictly speaking a simile) all vaunt the speed of Saracens' horses in alternate laisses, containing much *similaire* material and echo, in which some of the Twelve Peers die. The series at ll.3318-521, from the Baligant episode, denote the whiteness of beards. (For discussion and definitions of rhetorical figures, see Faral, *66*, Parr, *123*, esp. Appendix.)

The set-piece description of Turpin's horse (ll.1488-96) is a passage which shows the influence of the schools in more than one way. It has an *exordium* (ll.1488-89), an *elaboratio* (ll.1490-95) and an *epitome* (line 1496); the detailed description in the second of these is in a rigorous order, comparable to that of the model descriptions given in the *Artes poeticae* and followed by vernacular authors such as Chrétien (see Faral, *66*, pp.75-81; cf. *65*, pp.198-201, where a specific source in Book XII of Isidore of Seville's sixth-century *Etymologiae* is suggested). However, contrary to the models for human description and Isidore's horse paradigm, this one runs from the feet to the top of the head. The description of Baligant, ll.3155-64, has a very similar pattern, both as regards the three sections (respectively ll.3155-56, 3157-62, 3163-64) and the order of the *elaboratio*, which again goes from legs to head.

The foregoing review, in sum, shows a considerable volume of material which corresponds to figures of schoolman's rhetoric; but the formulaic tradition of epic (and, of course, much of what is picked out above finds parallels in other *chansons de geste*) produces convergences with formal rhetoric which leave some doubt as to how much of the material presupposes school, as opposed to epic, training. The question is not made easier by the fact that the *Roland* is probably the first extant specimen of its genre.

This last fact is significant also in connection with some final observations. One striking point is the relative richness in meaning of the text: many later epics tend (particularly when rhyme is substituted as an 'improvement' for assonance) to allow meaning to take refuge in the first hemistich, while a large proportion of second hemistichs are little more than line-fillers, used to produce the required rhyme. We are not yet at the stage of the ubiquitous *qui molt fist a prisier/loer* and *le baron al vis fier/fier vis*, etc., etc., though helmets and other pieces of equipment are already *gemmét ad or* (ll.1585, 1587), *a flurs e ad or* (line 1276), *as perres d'or gemmees* (line 1452), etc., rather automatically (to choose a few examples totally at random). Already the poet (foreshadowing a particular area of later abuse) allows himself to make frequent use of *estre* and *aler* followed by present participle to produce laisses in -*an*, particularly LXXXV, XCI, CXVI, CXXXIV, CLXXX, CCXLIX, but excessively only in XCI. Rare indeed are lame second hemistichs, the meaning of which is forced to provide an assonance, e.g. *ki que.l blasme ne qui.l lot*, line 1589, where praise or blame are quite inappropriate. It is true that there are many of the duplicating 'binomial' expressions so characteristic of later epics: *e de mort e de hunte*, line 21; *par honur e par ben*, line 39; *les mals ne les suffraites*, line 60; *li proz e li gentilz*, line 176; *merveilluse e comune*, line 1320; *e ferir e capler*, line 1681, and very many more. But such features are inherent in formulaic style, and in *Roland* they are nearly always fully appropriate to the context, and meaningful. This is rare in the genre, and it is matched by the ability to create lapidary, memorable, prestigious lines of poetry, especially at the end of laisses, of which a few examples may be found at the following subjectively chosen references: ll.1, 119, 178-79, 227, 285, 336, 716, 724+736, 814-15 (and variants on this motif), 1014-16, 1093-97, 1138, 1151, 1161, 1365-66, 1437, 1448, 1466, 1519-20, 1723, 1731, 1761-62, 1806, 1863-64, 1901, 1951, 2003-09, 2088, 2183, 2365, 2524, 2548+2554, 2658-59, 2854, 3120, 3164, 3513, 3519, 3578(+3914), 3611, 3657, 3717, 3723, 3872, 3959+3974, 4000-002. But in the last resort these lines and others achieve their resonance only in context; many, for example, enhance the tragedy by providing ominous premonition.

A surprising feature of a different kind is the considerable degree of consistency, at this period, in the use of *vouvoiement* and *tutoiement*. Though specialists in syntax no longer see twelfth century texts as showing complete arbitrariness in this matter (compare Foulet, *71*, para.289 with Moignet, *114*, p.262), and acquaintance with Chrétien de Troyes is enough to show that courtly authors could achieve very precise and subtle nuances from the distinction, other poets, such as Béroul, still make quite arbitrary changes long after 1100. In our poem, as Bédier saw (*32*, p.302) and as my own analysis, too complex to discuss here at length, confirms, there are few departures from what is to be expected if *vos/vus* (much the commoner) is already the pronoun of respect and *tu* that of familiarity, condescension and contempt. Thus the use of *tu* and *vus* by Ganelon and Roland respectively in the first nomination scene (ll.286-302) shows how the former is out of control, while the latter is coolly bating his stepfather with a show of reasonableness; Ganelon recovers enough to turn to *vus* at ll.306-07, after which he refers to Roland only in the third person. In the second nomination scene (ll.751-65), both men use *vouvoiement* for Roland's first, ironically courtly, reaction and Ganelon's answer, while the former's real contempt comes through with the change to *tu* for laisse LX. But this example will have to suffice here; and there are occasional lapses from consistency (among them approaches to the Deity) if one conducts a complete review.

There are other aspects of style which space forbids us to explore further, including the techniques by which the poet makes the narrative vivid, often almost visual; and, notably, the use of colour, light and sound, to which earlier chapters have made only episodic reference (see an excellent section in Cortés, *10*, pp.130-39, as well as Bennett, *34*). I hope enough has been said in this chapter to show, nevertheless, a very special talent at work at the stylistic level, to complement the grandiose, moving and penetrating conception of the subject which has been the object of analysis in the earlier chapters.

Bibliography

The following Bibliography consists mainly of editions and studies referred to in the text. For comprehensive coverage, consult the well-known *Manuel bibliographique de littérature française du moyen âge* of Robert Bossuat, with its *Suppléments 1949-1953, 1954-1960* (Melun, Librairie d'Argences, 1951-1961, also available in Slatkine Reprints, Geneva-Paris, 1986), now brought up to 1980 in the *Troisième Supplément 1960-1980*, by Françoise Vielliard and Jacques Monfrin, vol.I (Paris, Éditions du CNRS, 1986). This now overlaps usefully with Otto Klapp, *Bibliographie der französischen Literaturwissenschaft* 1- (Frankfurt am Main, Klostermann, 1960-). See also Joseph J. Duggan, *A Guide to Studies on the 'Chanson de Roland'*, Research Bibliographies and Checklists 15 (London, Grant & Cutler Ltd, 1976), and the *Bulletin bibliographique de la Société Rencesvals*, 1-22 (Paris, Nizet, 1958-1991) 23 (no place of publication given,1992), 24- (Université de Liège, 1993-).

Full bibliographical details of recurring conference *Acta* will be given only at the first occurrence, with short title and cross-reference thereafter.

EDITIONS OF THE 'CHANSON DE ROLAND'

1. T.D. Hemming (ed.), *La Chanson de Roland*. The Text of Frederick Whitehead revised, with a new introduction, bibliography and notes (Bristol, Bristol Classical Press, 1993). (Cf. 2.)
2. F. Whitehead (ed.), *La Chanson de Roland*. Blackwell's French Texts (Oxford, Basil Blackwell, 1942 and repr.). (Cf. 1.)
3. T. Atkinson Jenkins (ed.), *La Chanson de Roland: Oxford Version*. Edition, Notes, and Glossary, Heath's Modern Language Series (Boston, D.C.Heath and Co., 1924, revised 1929, reprinted 1954). (The notes are still very useful.)
4. J. Bédier (ed.), *La Chanson de Roland*, publiée d'après le manuscrit d'Oxford et traduite. Éd. définitive (Paris, Piazza, [1937]).
5. C. Segre (ed.), *La Chanson de Roland: Edizione critica*, Documenti di Filologia, XVI (Milan and Naples, Ricciardi, 1971). (Particularly valuable for its references to the whole manuscript tradition. Cf. 6.)

6. C. Segre (ed.), M. Tyssens (ed. and tr.), *La Chanson de Roland*. Nouvelle édition revue. Traduite de l'italien, Textes littéraires français, 368 (Geneva, Droz, 1989). (Cf. *5*; references, unless otherwise identified, will be to Vol. II.)

7. G. J. Brault (ed.), *The Song of Roland*. An analytical edition. Volume I. Introduction and Commentary. Volume II. Oxford Text and English Translation (University Park and London, Pennsylvania State University Press, 1978). (Extremely conservative edition, with sometimes tendentious translation. Very detailed and erudite commentaries of sometimes questionable applicability. References, unless otherwise identified, will be to Vol. I.)

8. G. Moignet (ed. and tr.), *La Chanson de Roland*. Texte original et traduction, Coll. Pour Connaître (Paris, Bordas, 3rd rev. edn, 1985; originally published 1969).

9. I. Short (ed. and tr.), *La Chanson de Roland*. Édition critique et traduction, Livre de Poche, Lettres Gothiques (Paris, Librairie Générale Française, 1990). (Interventionist edition, with many corrections; very useful translation, notes and introduction. 2nd revised edn printing at time of writing.)

10. Luis Cortés (ed.), Paulette Gabaudan (tr.), *La Chanson de Roland*. Édition établie d'après le manuscrit d'Oxford (Paris, Nizet, 1994). (This, very conservative, edition came to hand too late for systematic use here; it has an informative if sometimes simplistic, even misleading, introduction; useful textual notes; a translation into linguistically archaising French verse.)

11. R. Mortier (ed.), *Les Textes de la Chanson de Roland* (Paris, Éditions de la Geste Francor, 10 vols, 1940-44). (The only reasonably accessible attempt to publish the whole mediaeval *Roland* tradition, unfortunately not very accurately. The French manuscripts are currently being edited by an Anglo-American team co-ordinated by Joseph J. Duggan.)

TRANSLATIONS

Apart from those incorporated in some of the above editions, see also:

12. Burgess, Glyn, *The Song of Roland* (London, Penguin Classics, 1990).

13. Goldin, Frederick, *The Song of Roland* (New York, W.W. Norton & Co., 1978; quoted here mainly for its Introduction).

14. Owen, D.D.R., *The Song of Roland. The Oxford Text* (London, Unwin Books, 1972). (References are to this, out of print, edition; there is a new, augmented version (Woodbridge, Boydell Press, 1990) which I have not seen.)

EDITIONS OF OTHER MEDIAEVAL WORKS

15. *Buevon de Conmarchis*, ed. Albert Henry, *Les Oeuvres d'Adenet le Roi*, II (Bruges, 'De Tempel', 1953).
16. *Le Charroi de Nîmes. Chanson de geste du XIIe siècle*, ed. Duncan McMillan (2e éd. revue et corrigée, Paris, Klincksieck, 1978).
17. *Eneas. Roman du XIIe siècle*, ed. J.-J. Salverda de Grave (Paris, CFMA, 2 vols, 1925-29, repr. 1968).
18. *Gesta Francorum. The Deeds of the Franks and the Other Pilgrims to Jerusalem*, ed. Rosemary Hill (Oxford, Clarendon Press, 1962).
19. *Girart de Roussillon. Chanson de geste*, tr. Paul Meyer (Paris, Champion, 1884).
20. *Girart de Vienne par Bertrand de Bar-sur-Aube*, ed. Wolfgang van Emden (Paris, SATF, 1977).
21. *La Chanson de Guillaume*, ed. Duncan McMillan (Paris, SATF, 2 vols, 1949-50).
22. Marie de France, *Lais*, ed. Alfred Ewert, Blackwell's French Texts (Oxford, Basil Blackwell, 1944 and repr.).
23. *Raoul De Cambrai*. Edited with an Introduction, Translation and Notes by Sarah Kay (Oxford, Clarendon Press, 1992).
24. *La Chanson des Saisnes*, ed. Annette Brasseur (Geneva, Droz, TLF, 2 vols, 1989).
25. Thomas, *Les Fragments du Roman de Tristan*, ed. Bartina H. Wind (2nd edn, Geneva, Droz/Paris, Minard, TLF, 1960).

STUDIES

26. Aebischer, Paul, 'Pour la défense et illustration de l'épisode de Baligant', in *Mélanges de philologie romane et de littérature médiévale offerts à Ernest Hoepffner* (Paris, 'Les Belles Lettres', 1949), 173-82.
27. —, *Rolandiana et Oliveriana. Recueil d'études sur les chansons de geste*, Publications romanes et françaises, XCII (Geneva, Droz, 1967).
28. —, *Des Annales carolingiennes à Doon de Mayence. Nouveau recueil d'études sur l'épique française médiévale*, Publications romanes et françaises, CXXIX (Geneva, Droz, 1975).
29. Allen, John R., 'Du nouveau sur l'authenticité de l'épisode de Baligant', in *Actes du VIe Congrès International de la Société Rencesvals (Aix-en-Provence, 29 août - 4 septembre 1973)* (Aix-en-Provence, Université de Provence, 1974), 147-56.

30. Arthur, Ross G. 'The Baligant Episode in the *Chanson de Roland* and the *Historia* of Peter Tudebode', *Olifant*, 13 (3 & 4) (Fall & Winter 1988), 177-80.

31. Bédier, Joseph, *Les Légendes épiques. Recherches sur la formation des chansons de geste* (Paris, Champion, 4 vols, 1908-13, 2nd edn, 1914-21; 3rd edn, 1926-29, to which references are made in this monograph).

32. —, *La 'Chanson de Roland'. Commentaires,* (Paris, Piazza, 1927).

33. Bender, Karl-Heinz, *König und Vasall. Untersuchungen zur Chanson de Geste des XII. Jahrhunderts*, Studia Romanica, 13 (Heidelberg, Carl Winter. Universitätsverlag, 1967).

34. Bennett, Philip E., 'Further Reflections on the Luminosity of the Chanson de Roland', *Olifant*, 4 (3) (March 1977), 191-204.

35. Boatner, Janet, 'The Misunderstood Ordeal: a re-examination of the *Chanson de Roland'*, *Studies in Philology*, 66 (1969), 571-83.

36. Bowra, C. Maurice, *From Virgil to Milton* (London, Macmillan, 1945).

37. —, *Heroic Poetry* (London, Macmillan Papermac, 1964).

38. Braet, Herman, 'Le second rêve de Charlemagne dans la *Chanson de Roland*', *Romanica Gandensia*, 12 (1969), 5-19.

39. —, 'Le Brohun de la *Chanson de Roland*', *Zeitschrift für romanische Philologie*, 89 (1973), 97-102.

40. —, 'Le Songe dans la chanson de geste au XIIe siècle', *Romanica Gandensia*, 15 (1975), 9-251.

41. Brault, Gerard J., '*Sapientia* dans la *Chanson de Roland*', in *Proceedings of the Fifth Conference of the Société Rencesvals (Oxford 1970)* (University of Salford, 1977), 85-104.

42. Burger, André, 'Les deux scènes du cor dans la *Chanson de Roland*', in *La Technique littéraire des chansons de geste. Actes du Colloque de Liège (septembre 1957)*, (Paris, 'Les Belles Lettres', 1959), 105-26.

43. —, *Turold, poète de la fidélité. Essai d'explication de la 'Chanson de Roland'*, Publications romanes et françaises, CXLV (Geneva, Droz, 1977).

44. Burgess, Glyn, *Contribution à l'étude du vocabulaire pré-courtois* (Geneva, Droz, 1970).

45. —, 'Orgueil and Fierté in Twelfth-Century French', *Zeitschrift für romanische Philologie*, 89 (1973), 103-22.

46. —, 'Remarques sur deux vers de la *Chanson de Roland* (vv. 3796-7)', in *Rencesvals VI* (see *29*), 65-78.

47. Calin, William C., 'L'épopée dite vivante: Réflexions sur le prétendu caractère oral des chansons de geste', *Olifant*, 8 (3) (Spring 1981), 227-37.

48. —, 'Littérature médiévale et hypothèse orale: une divergence de méthode et de philosophie', *ibid.*, 256-85. (Cf. Duggan articles *57, 58* in same number of *Olifant*: this was a debate organised by the review.)

49. Cartier, Normand R., 'La Sagesse de Roland', *Aquila. Chestnut Hill Studies in Modern Languages and Literatures,* 1 (1968), 33-63.

50. Cook, Robert F., *The Sense of the 'Song of Roland'* (Ithaca and London, Cornell University Press, 1987).

51. Crist, Larry S., 'A propos de la *desmesure* dans la *Chanson de Roland*: quelques propos (démesurés?)', *Olifant*, 1 (4) (April 1974), 10-20. (Also in *Rencesvals V* (see *41*), 143-55.)

52. Curtius, Ernst Robert, *European Literature and the Latin Middle Ages*, tr. Willard R. Trask (London, Routledge and Kegan Paul, 1953; first published in German, Berne, Francke, 1948).

53. Delbouille, Maurice, *Sur la genèse de la 'Chanson de Roland' (Travaux récents – Propositions nouvelles). Essai critique* (Bruxelles, Palais des Académies, 1954).

54. —, 'Les chansons de geste et le livre', in *Technique littéraire* (see *42*), 295-407.

55. Duggan, Joseph J., *The 'Song of Roland'. Formulaic style and poetic craft* (Berkeley, Los Angeles, London, University of California Press, 1973).

56. —, 'The Generation of the Episode of Baligant', *Romance Philology*, 30 (1976), 59-82.

57. —, 'La Théorie de la Composition orale des chansons de geste: les faits et les interprétations', *Olifant*, 8 (1) (Spring 1981), 238-55.

58. —, 'Le Mode de composition des chansons de geste: Analyse statistique, jugement esthétique, modèles de transmission', *ibid.*, 286-316. (Cf. Calin, *47, 48*.)

59. —, 'El juicio de Ganelón y el mito del pecado de Carlomagno en la versión de Oxford de la *Chanson de Roland*', Joan Ramón Resina, ed., *Mythopoesis: Literatura, totalidad, ideología* (Barcelona, Anthropos, 1992), 53-64.

60. Dunbabin, Jean, *France in the Making 843-1180* (Oxford, University Press, 1985).

61. Edge, David, and Paddock, John Miles, *Arms and Armour of the Medieval Knight* (London, Guild Publishing, 1988).

62. Eichmann, Raymond, 'Oral Composition. A recapitulatory view of its nature and impact', *Neuphilologische Mitteilungen*, 80 (1979), 97-109.

63. Elliott, Alison Goddard, 'The *Vie de Saint Alexis*: oral versus written style', in *VIII Congreso de la Société Rencesvals. Pamplona - Santiago de Compostela. 15 a 25 de agosto de 1978* (Pamplona, Diputacion Foral de Navarra, 1981), 137-48.

64. —, 'The Double Genesis of *Girart de Vienne*', *Olifant*, 8 (2) (Winter 1980), 130-60.

65. Faral, Edmond, *Recherches sur les sources latines des contes et romans courtois du moyen âge* (Paris, Champion, 1913, repr. 1967).

66. —, *Les Arts poétiques du XIIe et du XIIIe siècle* (Paris, Champion, 1924).

67. —, *La Chanson de Roland. Étude et analyse*, Les Chefs d'oeuvre de la littérature expliqués (Paris, Mellottée, 1933 and repr.).

68. Finnegan, Ruth, *Oral Poetry. Its nature, significance and social context* (Cambridge University Press, 1977, paperback, 1979).

69. Folz, Robert, *Le Souvenir et la légende de Charlemagne dans l'empire germanique médiéval* (Paris, 'Les Belles Lettres', 1950).

70. Foulet, Alfred, 'Is Roland Guilty of *Desmesure?*', *Romance Philology*, 10 (1957), 145-48.

71. Foulet, Lucien, *Petite syntaxe de l'ancien français* (Paris, CFMA, 3rd edn, 1928, repr. 1930).

72. Ganshof, F.L., *Feudalism*, 3rd English edn, tr. from French by Philip Grierson (London, Longmans, 1964).

73. Gautier, Léon, *Les Épopées françaises* (Paris, V. Palmé, 3 vols,1865-68; 2nd edn, 4 vols, 1878-92).

74. Gougenheim, Georges, 'Orgueil et fierté dans la *Chanson de Roland*', in *Mélanges... offerts à Jean Frappier...* (Geneva, Droz, 2 vols, 1970), vol. I, 365-73.

75. Guiette, Robert, 'Les Deux Scènes du cor dans la *Chanson de Roland* et dans les *Conquestes de Charlemagne*', *Le Moyen Age*, 69 (1963), 845-55.

76. Hackett, W. Mary, 'Le Gant de Roland', *Romania*, 89 (1968), 253-56.

77. Hecht (cf. Holland), Michael, *La Chanson de Turold. Essai de déchiffrement de la 'Chanson de Roland'* (Paris, J.C. Bailly, 1988).

78. Heinemann, Edward A., 'Composition stylisée et technique littéraire dans la *Chanson de Roland*', *Romania*, 94 (1973), 1-28.

79. —, 'La Composition stylisée et la transmission écrite des textes rolandiens', in *Rencesvals VI* (see *29*), 255-72.

80. —, *L'Art métrique de la chanson de geste. Essai sur la musicalité du récit*, Publications romanes et françaises, CCV (Geneva, Droz, 1993).

81. Hemming, Timothy D., review of H.E. Keller, *Autour de Roland* (cf. *92*), *French Studies*, 45 (1991), 450.

82. Hoepffner, Ernest, 'Les rapports littéraires entre les premières chansons de geste', *Studi medievali*, 4 (n.s.) (1931), 233-58 and VI (n.s.) (1933), 45-81.

83. Holland (cf. Hecht), Michael, 'Rolandus resurrectus', in Pierre Gallais and Yves-Jean Riou (eds), *Mélanges offerts à René Crozet* (Société d'Études Médiévales, Poitiers, 1966), 397-418.

84. Horrent, Jules, *La 'Chanson de Roland' dans les littératures française et espagnole au moyen âge* (Paris, 'Les Belles Lettres', 1951).

85. Hunt, Tony, 'Character and Causality in the Oxford *Roland*', *Medioevo Romanzo*, 5 (1978), 3-33.

86. —, 'The Tragedy of Roland: an Aristotelian view', *Modern Language Review*, 74 (1979), 791-805.

87. —, 'Roland's "Vermeille Pume"', *Olifant*, 7 (3) (Spring 1980), 203-11.

88. Jones, George Fenwick, *The Ethos of the 'Song of Roland'* (Baltimore, Johns Hopkins Press, 1963).

89. Jonin, Pierre, 'Deux langages de héros épiques au cours d'une bataille suicidaire', *Olifant*, 9 (3 & 4) (Spring & Summer 1982), 83-98.

90. Kay, Sarah, 'Ethics and Heroics in the *Song of Roland*', *Neophilologus*, 62 (1978), 480-91.

91. —, 'The Epic Formula: a revised definition', *Zeitschrift für französische Sprache und Literatur*, 93 (1983), 170-89.

92. Keller, Hans-Erich, *Autour de Roland. Recherches sur la chanson de geste* (Paris, Champion, 1989).

93. Keen, Maurice, *Chivalry* (New Haven and London, Yale University Press, 1984).

94. Kern, Fritz, *Gottesgnadentum und Widerstandsrecht im früheren Mittelalter. Zur Entwicklungsgeschichte der Monarchie* (Darmstadt, Wissenschaftliche Buchgesellschaft, repr. of 2nd edn (1954), 1973).

95. Kibler, William W., 'Roland's Pride', *Symposium*, 26 (1972), 147-57.

96. —, 'Roland and Tierri', *Olifant*, 2 (1) (October 1974), 27-32. (Cf. *160.*)

97. Knudson, Charles, 'La Brogne', in *Mélanges offerts à Rita Lejeune* (Gembloux, Éditions J. Duculot, 2 vols, 1969), II, 1625-35.

98. Kullmann, Dorothea, *Verwandschaft in epischer Dichtung. Untersuchungen zu den französischen 'chansons de geste' und Romanen des 12. Jahrhunderts*, Beihefte zur Zeitschrift für romanische Philologie, 242 (Tübingen, Max Niemeyer Verlag, 1992).

99. Labande, Edmond-René, 'Le Credo épique', in *Recueil de travaux offerts à M. Clovis Brunel* (Paris, S.E.C., 2 vols, 1955), II, 62-80.

100. Le Gentil, Pierre, 'La Notion d'état latent', *Bulletin hispanique*, 55 (1953), 113-48.

101. —, *La Chanson de Roland*, Connaissance des lettres (Paris, Hatier, 2nd rev. edn, 1967).

102. —, 'A propos de la démesure de Roland', *Cahiers de Civilisation Médiévale*, 11 (1968), 203-09.

103. Lejeune, Rita, 'La Naissance du couple littéraire "Roland et Olivier"', in *Mélanges Henri Grégoire*, Annuaire de l'Institut de Philologie et d'Histoire Orientales et Slaves, 10 (2 vols, 1950), II, 371-401.

104. Lord, Albert Bates, *The Singer of Tales*, Harvard Studies in
       Comparative Literature, 24 (Harvard University Press, 1960;
       paperback printing New York, Atheneum, 1965, 4th printing 1971).

105. Louis, René, *De l'histoire à la légende* (Auxerre, Imprimerie
       Moderne, 3 vols, 1946-47).

106. —, 'Avant-propos. Qu'est-ce que l'épopée vivante?', *La Table Ronde,*
       132 (décembre 1958), 9-17.

107. Lyons, Faith, 'More about Roland's glove', in *Rencesvals V* (see *41*),
       156-66.

108. Magoun, Francis P., 'Oral-Formulaic Character of Anglo-Saxon
       Narrative Poetry', *Speculum*, 28 (1953), 446-67.

109. Mayer, Hans Eberhard, *The Crusades* (Oxford, University Press, 2nd
       edn, 1988).

110. Mickel, Emanuel J., *Ganelon, Treason and the 'Chanson de Roland'*
       (University Park and London, Pennsylvania State University Press,
       1989).

111. Mireaux, Émile, *La 'Chanson de Roland' et l'histoire de France*
       (Paris, Éditions Albin Michel, 1943).

112. Misrahi, Jean, and Hendrickson, William L., 'Roland and Oliver:
       prowess and wisdom, the ideal of the epic hero', *Romance Philology,*
       33 (1980), 357-72. (Cf. *113*.)

113. —, 'L'Idéal du héros épique: prouesse et sagesse', in *Rencesvals VIII*
       (see *63*), 223-31. (cf.*112*.)

114. Moignet, Gérard, *Grammaire de l'ancien français. Morphologie –*
       Syntaxe (Paris, Klincksieck, 2nd rev. edn 1979).

115. Mölk, Ulrich, 'Rolands Schuld', in Susanne Knaller and Edith Mara,
       (eds), *Das Epos in der Romania. Festschrift für Dieter Kremers zum*
       65. Geburtstag (Tübingen, Gunter Narr Verlag, 1986), 299-308.

116. Morris, Colin, '*Judicium Dei*: the social and political significance of
       the ordeal in the eleventh century', *Studies in Church History*, 12
       (Oxford, 1975), pp.95-111.

117. Nottarp, Hermann, *Gottesurteilstudien,* Bamberger Abhandlungen und
       Forschungen, II (München, I.M. Kosel-Verlag, 1956).

118. Owen, D.D. Roy, 'The Secular Inspiration of the *Chanson de Roland*',
       Speculum, 37 (1962), 390-400.

119. —, 'Charlemagne's Dreams, Baligant and Turoldus', *Zeitschrift für*
       romanische Philologie, 87 (1971), 197-208.

120. —, 'Aspects of *desmesure* (*Chanson de Roland, Raoul de Cambrai,*
       Girart de Roussillon)', in Linda M. Paterson and Simon B. Gaunt
       (eds), *The Troubadours and the Epic. Essays in memory of W. Mary*
       Hackett, (The University of Warwick, Department of French, 1987),
       pp.143-68.

121. Paris, Gaston, *Histoire poétique de Charlemagne* (Paris, Franck,1865; new ed., Paris, Bouillon, 1905).

122. —, *Extraits de la 'Chanson de Roland'* (Paris, 2nd edn, 1889).

123. Parr, Roger P. (ed.), *Geoffrey of Vinsauf. Documentum de modo et arte dictandi et versificandi* (Milwaukee, Wisconsin, Marquette U.P., 1968).

124. Parry, Milman, and Lord, Albert Bates, *Serbocroatian Heroic Songs. I. Novi Pazar: English translations* (Cambridge, Mass., and Belgrade, Harvard University Press and Serbian Academy of Sciences, 2 vols, 1954 and 1953).

125. Pauphilet, Albert, *Le Legs du moyen âge. Études de littérature médiévale* (Paris, Librairie d'Argences, 1950).

126. Payen, Jean-Charles, *Le Motif du repentir dans la littérature française médiévale (des origines à 1230)*, Publications romanes et françaises, XCVIII (Geneva, Droz, 1968).

127. Pensom, Roger, *Literary Technique in the 'Chanson de Roland'* (Geneva, Droz, 1982).

128. Pfeffer, M., 'Die Formalitäten des gottesgerichtlichen Zweikampfs in der altfranzösischen Epik', *Zeitschrift für romanische Philologie*, 9 (1885), 1-74.

129. Picherit, Jean-Louis, 'Le Silence de Ganelon', *Cahiers de Civilisation Médiévale*, 21 (1978), 265-74.

130. Pidal, Ramón Menéndez, *La Chanson de Roland et la tradition épique des Francs*, tr. from Spanish by I.-M. Cluzel (Paris, Picard, 1960).

131. Rajna, Pio, *Le origini dell'epopea francese* (Florence, Sansoni, 1884).

132. Reed, J., 'The "Bref" in the *Chanson de Roland*', *French Studies Bulletin*, 39 (Summer 1991), 3-7.

133. Renoir, Alain, 'Roland's Lament: its meaning and function in the *Chanson de Roland*', *Speculum*, 35 (1960), 572-83.

134. Riquer, Martín de, *Les Chansons de geste françaises*, 2nd edn tr. by Irénée Cluzel (Paris, Nizet, [1957], repr. 1968).

135. Robertson, D.W., Jr., *A Preface to Chaucer. Studies in medieval perspectives* (Princeton, New Jersey, Princeton U.P., 1969).

136. Ross, David J.A., 'Before *Roland*: what happened 1200 years ago next August 15?', *Olifant*, 5 (3) (March 1978), 171-90.

137. Ruggieri, Ruggero M., *Il processo di Gano nella 'Chanson de Roland'*, (Florence, Sansoni, 1936).

138. Rychner, Jean, *La Chanson de geste. Essai sur l'art épique des jongleurs*, Publications romanes et françaises, LIII (Geneva, Droz, and Lille, Giard, 1955).

139. —, 'La chanson de geste, épopée vivante', *La Table Ronde*, 132 (décembre 1958), 152-67.

140. Samaran, Charles, *La Chanson de Roland. Reproduction phototypique du manuscrit Digby 23 de la Bodleian Library d'Oxford.* Édition avec un avant-propos par le comte Alexandre de Laborde. Étude paléographique de M. Charles Samaran (Paris, SATF, 1933).

141. —, 'Sur la date approximative du Roland d'Oxford', *Romania*, 94 (1973), 523-27.

142. Scully, Terence, 'The Ordeal at Roncesvalles: *Francs e paiens, as les vus ajustez*', *Olifant*, 7 (3) (Spring 1980), 213-34.

143. Short, Ian, 'The Oxford Manuscript of the *Chanson de Roland*: a palaeographic note', *Romania*, 94 (1973), 221-31.

144. Siciliano, Italo, *François Villon et les thèmes poétiques du moyen-âge* (Paris, Nizet, 1934, repr. 1967).

145. Spraycar, Rudy S., '*La Chanson de Roland*: an oral poem?', *Olifant*, 4 (1) (October 1976), 63-70.

146. Steinmeyer, Karl-Joseph, *Untersuchungen zur allegorischen Bedeutung der Träume im altfranzösischen Rolandslied* (Munich, Hüber,1963).

147. Stowell, William A., 'Personal Relationships in Medieval France', *Publications of the Modern Language Association of America*, 28 (1913), 388-416.

148. Suard, François, *La Chanson de geste*, Que sais-je? (Paris, PUF, 1993).

149. Sutherland, D. Rhoda, 'Les vers 1710 et 1711 dans la version d'Oxford de la *Chanson de Roland*', in *Rencesvals V* (see *41*), 1-4.

150. Uitti, Karl D., *Old French Narrative Poetry, 1050-1200* (Princeton, N.J., Princeton U.P., 1973).

151. Ullmann, Walter, *Principles of Government and Politics in the Middle Ages* (London, Methuen, 2nd edn,1966).

152. Vance, Eugene, *Reading the 'Song of Roland'* (Englewood Cliffs, N.J., Prentice-Hall, Inc., 1970).

153. van der Veen, J., 'Les aspects musicaux des chansons de geste', *Neophilologus*, 41 (1957), 82-100.

154. van Emden, Wolfgang G., 'Isembart and the Old French Epic of Revolt', *Nottingham Mediaeval Studies*, 8 (1964), 22-34.

155. —, '"La bataille est aduree endementres": traditionalism and individualism in chanson-de-geste studies', *Nottingham Mediaeval Studies, 13* (1969), 3-26.

156. —, 'Rolandiana et Oliveriana. Faits et hypothèses', *Romania*, 92 (1971), 507-31.

157. —, '"E cil de France le cleiment a guarant": Roland, Vivien et le thème du guarant', *Olifant*, 1 (4) (April 1974), 21-47. (Also in *Rencesvals VI* (see *29*), 33-61.)

158. —, 'Another Look at Charlemagne's Dreams in the *Chanson de Roland*', *French Studies*, 28 (1974), 257-71.

159. —, 'Pro Karolo Magno: in response to William W. Kibler, "Roland and Tierri"', *Olifant* 2 (3) (February 1975), 175-82. (Cf. *96.*)

160. —, 'Trial by Ordeal and Combat: the deliquescence of a motif', in Christopher Thacker (ed.), *Essays for Peter Mayer* (Reading, The University, 1980), 173-93.

161. —, '*Girart de Vienne* devant les ordinateurs', in André Moisoan (ed.), *La chanson de geste et le mythe carolingien. Mélanges René Louis* (Saint-Père-sous-Vézelay, 1982), 663-690.

162. —, '*Argumentum ex Silentio*: an aspect of dramatic technique in *La Chanson de Roland*', *Romance Philology*, 43 (1989), 181-96.

163. —, review of Hans-Erich Keller, *Autour de Roland* (cf. *92*), *Medium Aevum*, 60 (1991), 311-12.

164. —, 'Kingship in the Old French Epic of Revolt', in Anne J. Duggan (ed.), *Kings and Kingship in Medieval Europe*, King's College London Medieval Studies, X (King's College London Centre for Late Antique and Medieval Studies, 1993), 305-50.

165. —, 'The reception of Roland in some Old French epics', to appear in the *Acta* of the 'Roland in Europe' Symposium, London, May 1993, to be edited by Karen Pratt in the King's College London Medieval Studies Series.

166. —, 'La Réception du personnage de Roland dans quelques oeuvres plus ou moins épiques des 12e, 13e et 14e siècles', to appear in the *Acta* of the XIIIth International Conference of the Société Rencesvals, Groningen, August 1994.

167. Venckeleer, Theo, *Rollant li proz. Contribution à l'histoire de quelques qualifications laudatives en français du moyen âge* (Lille, Atelier Reproduction des Thèses, Université Lille III; Paris, Champion, 1975).

168. Vinaver, Eugène, 'La mort de Roland', in *A la recherche d'une poétique médiévale* (Paris, Nizet, 1970), 49-74 (also in *Cahiers de Civilisation Médiévale*, 7 (1964), 133-43).

169. Walker, Roger M., '"Tere major" in the *Chanson de Roland*', *Olifant* 4 (2) (December 1976), 123-30.

170. Walpole, Ronald N., 'The *Nota Emilianense*. New light (but how much?) on the origins of the Old French epic', *Romance Philology*, 10 (1957), 1-18.

171. Whitehead, Frederick, 'Charlemagne's Second Dream', *Olifant*, 3 (3) (March 1976), 189-95.

172. Zink, Michel, *Littérature française du moyen âge* (Paris, PUF, 1992).

173. Zumthor, Paul, 'Étude typologique des *planctus* conténus dans la *Chanson de Roland*', in *Technique littéraire* (see *42*), 219-35.

CRITICAL GUIDES TO FRENCH TEXTS

edited by
Roger Little, Wolfgang van Emden, David Williams